国务院侨务办公室
中国海外交流协会

Common Knowledge about Chinese Geography

The Overseas Chinese Affairs Office of the State Council
China Overseas Exchanges Association

前言

《中国历史常识》、《中国地理常识》和《中国文化常识》是中华人民共和国国务院侨务办公室、中国海外交流协会委托南京师范大学、安徽师范大学和北京华文学院分别编写的一套华文教学辅助读物，供海外华裔青少年通过课堂学习或自学的方式了解中国历史、地理、文化常识，也可供家长辅导孩子学习使用。我们希望学习者通过学习，初步了解、掌握中国历史、地理和文化的知识，进而达到普及、弘扬中华文化和促进中外文化交流的目的。

根据海外华文教学的实际情况和需求，我们分别选编了中国历史的重大事件和重要人物，进行客观记述；选取了中国地理最主要的自然特点和人文特征，进行概略描述；筛选了中华文化和民俗风情的精华，加以介绍。突出体现科学性、思想性和实用性的编写原则，在编排设计等方面力求有所创新。

在上述三本书的编写过程中，苏寿桐、王宏志、臧嵘、侯明、刘淑英、李芳芹等参加了《中国历史常识》的审稿工作；王永昌、乐平兰、刘淑梅、毕超、徐玉奎、董乃灿、张桂珠、李文君等参加了《中国地理常识》的审稿工作；张英、张猛、董明、武惠华、陶卫、杨二林等参加了《中国文化常识》的审稿工作。在此，谨表示诚挚的谢意。

书中考虑不周或疏漏之处，祈盼使用者不吝赐正，以期再版时修订。

编　者

2001年12月

Preface

The Overseas Chinese Affairs Office of the State Council of the People's Republic of China and China Overseas Exchanges Association commissioned Nanjing Normal University, Anhui Normal University and Beijing Chinese Language College to respectively write this set of auxiliary Chinese language teaching materials, namely, *Common Knowledge about Chinese History*, *Common Knowledge about Chinese Geography* and *Common Knowledge about Chinese Culture* which acquaint overseas Chinese teenagers with basic knowledge on these subjects through class education or self-teaching. Parents can also use them to help their children with study. Moreover, we hope this set of books can offer a wider group of readers some rudimentary knowledge about Chinese history, geography and culture, thus promoting cultural exchanges between China and other countries.

According to the actual condition and needs of overseas Chinese language teaching, in this set of books, we objectively narrate important events and figures in Chinese history; briefly describe the major natural and cultural features of Chinese geography; carefully select and introduce the essence of the Chinese culture, habits and customs. We have tried to introduce new ideas in typesetting, design and so on and to embody scientific, ideological and practical principles in the writing.

We are deeply grateful to Su Shoutong, Wang Hongzhi, Zang Rong, Hou Ming, Liu Shuying and Li Fangqin for revising *Common Knowledge about Chinese History*, Wang Yongchang, Yue Pinglan, Liu Shumei, Bi Chao, Xu Yukui, Dong Naican, Zhang Guizhu and Li Wenjun for revising *Common Knowledge about Chinese Geography*, and Zhang Ying, Zhang Meng, Dong Ming, Wu Huihua, Tao Wei and Yang Erlin for revising *Common Knowledge about Chinese Culture.*

Advice is welcomed if there were any mistake in the books. We will revise them when republishing the books.

Compilers

December, 2001

目录 Contents

中国概览
A General Survey of China

锦绣河山
Land of Charm and Beauty

山脉 Mountains

高原 Plateaus

目录 Contents

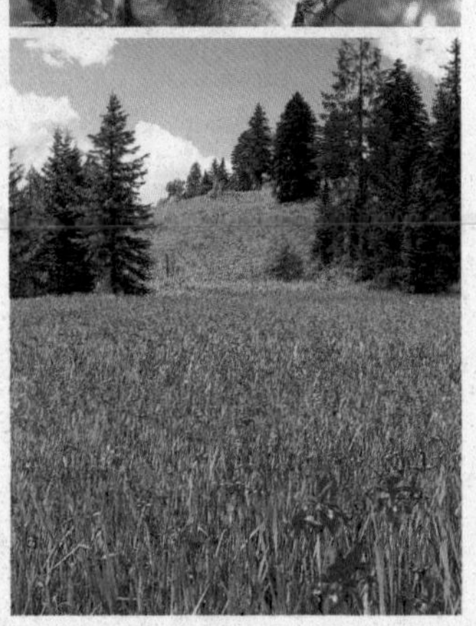

交通与水利
Transportation and Water Conservancy

资源与环境
Resources and Environment

历史名城与现代都市
Famous Historical Cities and Modern Cities

旅游胜地
Tourist Attractions

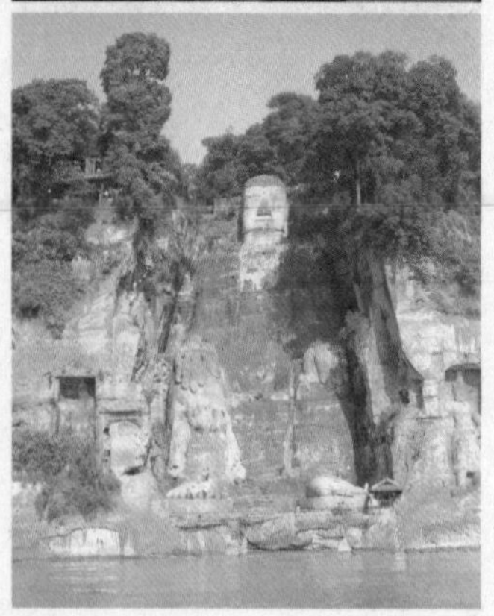

附录1 Appendix I

附录2 Appendix II

中国概览

A General Survey of China

中国的地理位置
Location of China in the World

中国位于欧亚大陆的东部，太平洋的西岸。中国的陆上疆界长达20,000多千米，拥有15个邻国。

Located in the east of the Asia-Europe Continent, on the western shore of the Pacific Ocean, China has a land boundary of some 20,000 km, with 15 neighboring countries.

中国的地形复杂多样

China has a diverse topography.

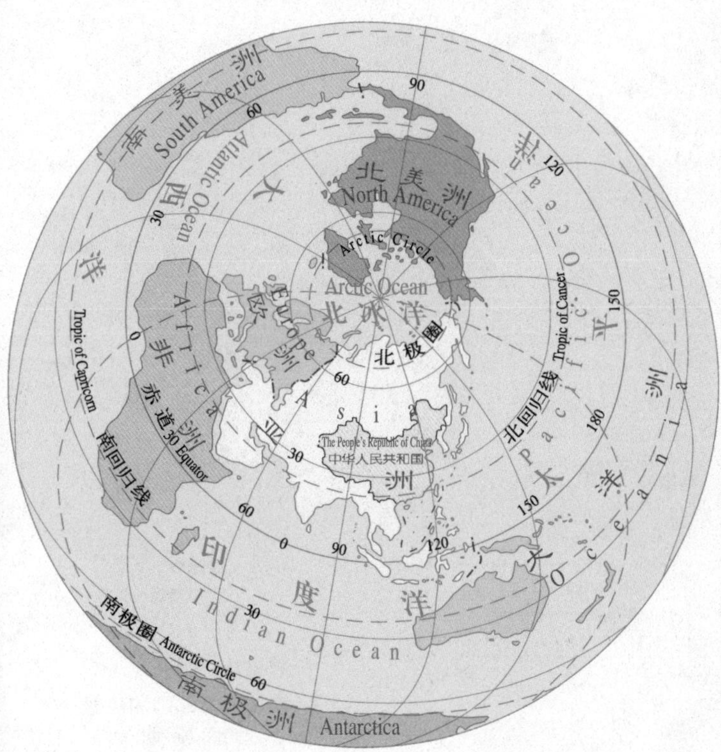

中国的地理位置

Location of China in the World

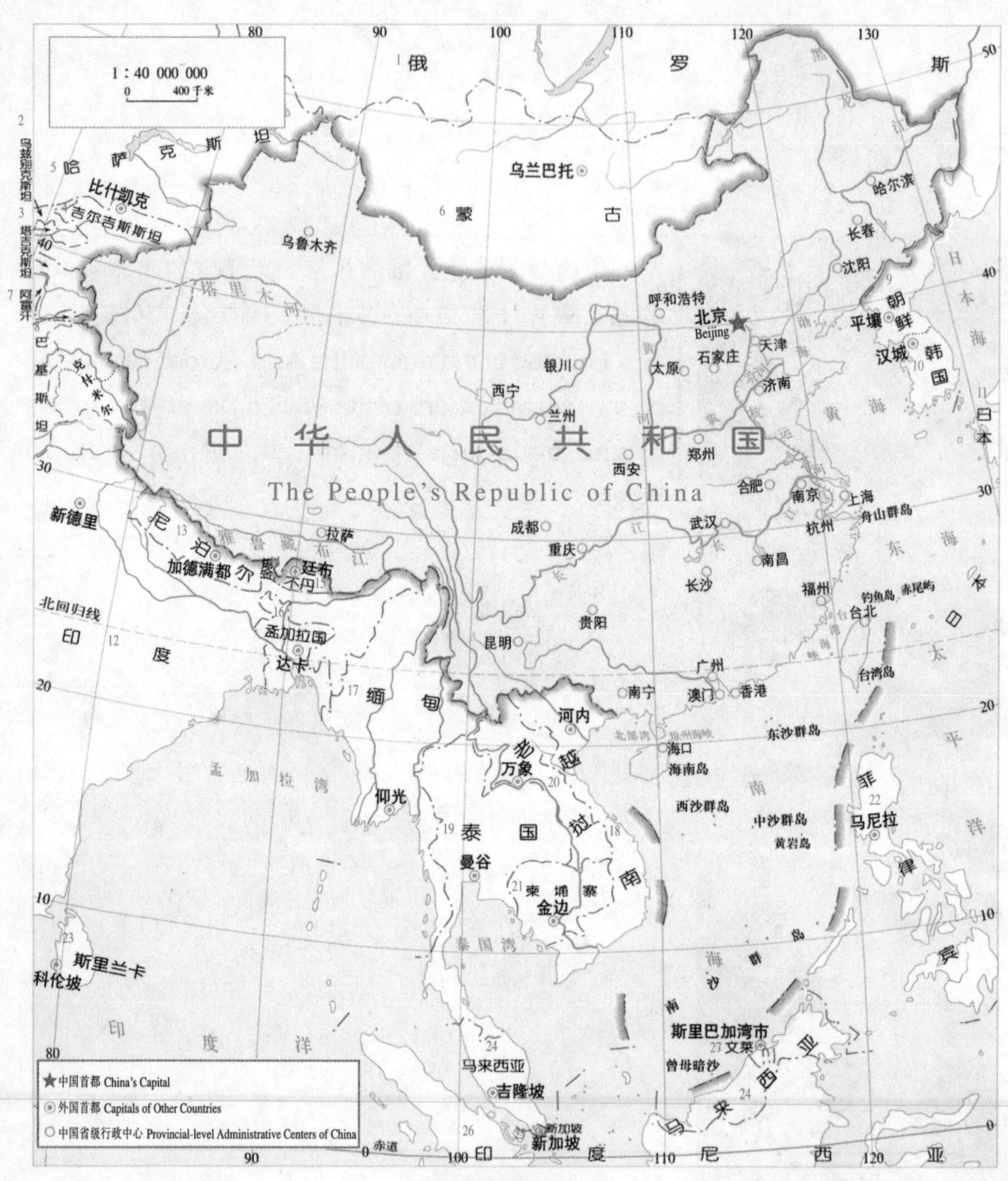

中国及其邻国的位置

China's Neighbors

中国的邻国及其首都
China's Neighbor Countries and Their Capitals

	邻国 Countries	首都 Capitals
1	俄罗斯 Russia	莫斯科 Moscow
2	乌兹别克斯坦 Uzbekistan	塔什干 Tashkent
3	塔吉克斯坦 Tajikistan	杜尚别 Dushanbe
4	吉尔吉斯斯坦 Kyrgyzstan	比什凯克 Bishkek
5	哈萨克斯坦 Kazakhstan	阿斯塔纳 Astana
6	蒙古 Mongolia	乌兰巴托 Ulan Bator
7	阿富汗 Afghanistan	喀布尔 Kabul
8	巴基斯坦 Pakistan	伊斯兰堡 Islamabad
9	朝鲜 The Democratic People's Republic of Korea	平壤 Pyongyang
10	韩国 The Republic of Korea	汉城 Seoul
11	日本 Japan	东京 Tokyo
12	印度 India	新德里 New Delhi
13	尼泊尔 Nepal	加德满都 Kathmandu
14	锡金 Sikkim	甘托克 Gangtok
15	不丹 Bhutan	廷布 Thimphu
16	孟加拉国 Bangladesh	达卡 Dhaka
17	缅甸 Myanmar	仰光 Yangon
18	越南 Vietnam	河内 Hanoi
19	泰国 Thailand	曼谷 Bangkok
20	老挝 Laos	万象 Vientiane
21	柬埔寨 Cambodia	金边 Phnom Penh
22	菲律宾 The Philippines	马尼拉 Manila
23	斯里兰卡 Sri Lanka	科伦坡 Colombo
24	马来西亚 Malaysia	吉隆坡 Kuala Lumpur
25	新加坡 Singapore	新加坡 Singapore
26	印度尼西亚 Indonesia	雅加达 Jakarta
27	文莱 Brunei	斯里巴加湾市 Bandar Seri Begawan

黄河流入渤海前形成大片三角洲湿地

The delta wetland is formed by the Yellow River emptying into the Bohai Sea.

大陆海岸线北起中朝边界的鸭绿江口，南到中越边界的北仑河口，总长18,000多千米。濒临渤海、黄海、东海、南海四大海域。沿海分布着5,000多个岛屿，台湾岛是中国的第一大岛。岛屿海岸线长14,000千米。

China's mainland coastline extends from the Yalu River on the border with North Korea in the north to the Beilun River on the border of China and Vietnam in the south, measuring approximately 18,000 km. The Chinese mainland is flanked to the east and south by the Bohai, Yellow, East China and South China seas. A total of over 5,000 islands dot China's territorial waters. The largest of these is Taiwan. The island coastline measures approximately 14,000 km.

小资料 Data

中国东邻朝鲜，东北部、北部和西北部与俄罗斯、蒙古、哈萨克斯坦、吉尔吉斯斯坦、塔吉克斯坦相邻，西部和西南部毗邻阿富汗、巴基斯坦、印度、尼泊尔、锡金、不丹，南接越南、老挝、缅甸。

China is bordered by Korea to the east; Mongolia to the north; Russia to the northeast; Kazakhstan, Kyrgyzstan and Tajikistan to the northwest; Afghanistan, Pakistan, India, Nepal, Sikkim and Bhutan to the west and southwest; and Vietnam, Laos and Myanmar to the south.

你知道吗 Do you know

同中国隔海相望的国家有日本、韩国、菲律宾、马来西亚、印度尼西亚和文莱。

Across the seas to the east and southeast of China are Japan, the Republic of Korea, the Philippines, Malaysia, Indonesia and Brunei.

在中国的版图上
Territory

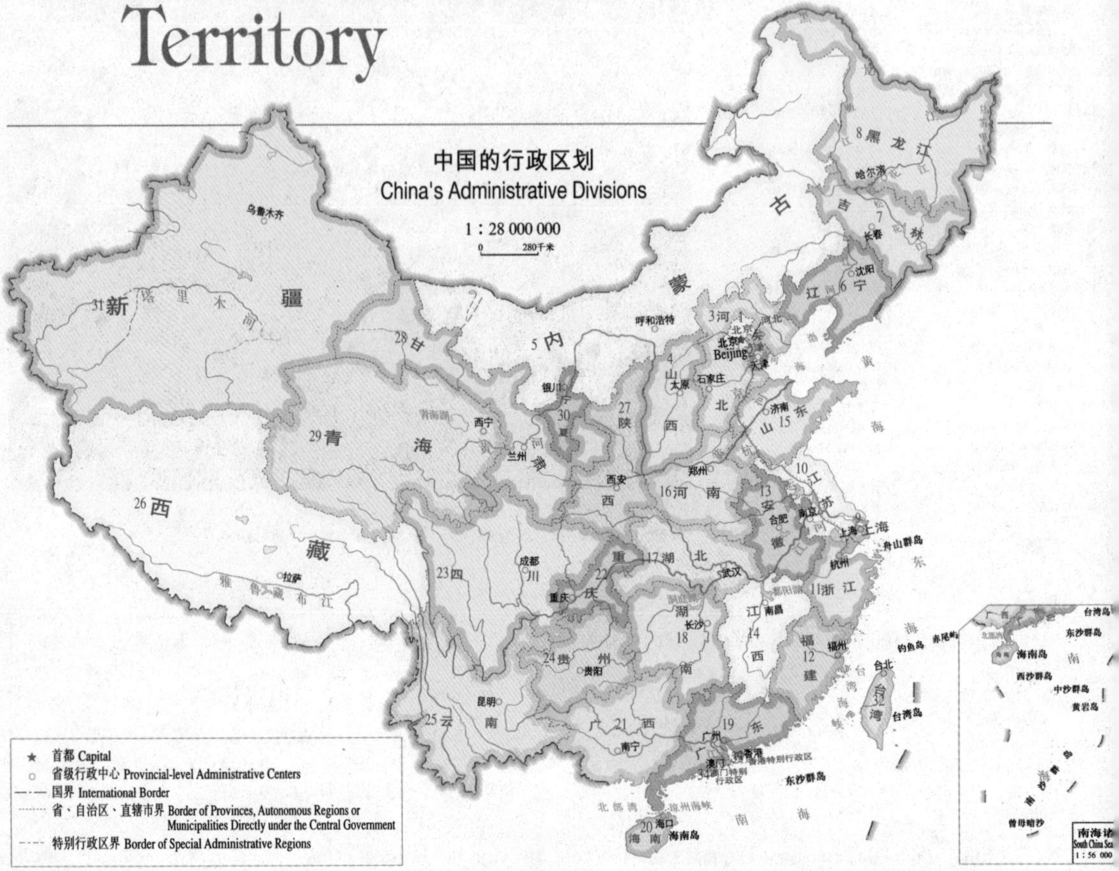

中国的行政区划
China's Administrative Divisions

1 : 28 000 000

0 280千米

★ 首都 Capital
○ 省级行政中心 Provincial-level Administrative Centers
—·— 国界 International Border
------ 省、自治区、直辖市界 Border of Provinces, Autonomous Regions or Municipalities Directly under the Central Government
- - - 特别行政区界 Border of Special Administrative Regions

中国领土的最北端是黑龙江省漠河以北的黑龙江主航道中心线，最南端是南沙群岛的曾母暗沙。南北跨50个纬度左右，相距5,500千米。当东北进入隆冬季节的时候，南方的海南岛依然是一片夏季的景象。

From north to south, the territory of China spans over 50° of latitude, stretching from the center of the Heilongjiang River north of the town of Mohe of Heilongjiang Province to the Zengmu Reef at the southernmost tip of the South Sand Islands. China extends 5,500 km from north to south. When the northeast of China is plunged into winter, Hainan Island in the south still enjoys summer.

中国各省、自治区、直辖市简表
Provinces, Autonomous Regions and Municipalities Directly under the Central Government

序号 No.	全称 Full Name	简称 Abbreviation	行政中心 Administration Center
1	北京市 Beijing	京 Jing	北京 Beijing
2	天津市 Tianjin	津 Jin	天津 Tianjin
3	河北省 Hebei Province	冀 Ji	石家庄 Shijiazhuang
4	山西省 Shanxi Province	晋 Jin	太原 Taiyuan
5	内蒙古自治区 Inner Mongolia Autonomous Region	内蒙古 Inner Mongolia	呼和浩特 Hohhot
6	辽宁省 Liaoning Province	辽 Liao	沈阳 Shenyang
7	吉林省 Jilin Province	吉 Ji	长春 Changchun
8	黑龙江省 Heilongjiang Province	黑 Hei	哈尔滨 Harbin
9	上海市 Shanghai	沪 Hu	上海 Shanghai
10	江苏省 Jiangsu Province	苏 Su	南京 Nanjing
11	浙江省 Zhejiang Province	浙 Zhe	杭州 Hangzhou
12	福建省 Fujian Province	闽 Min	福州 Fuzhou
13	安徽省 Anhui Province	皖 Wan	合肥 Hefei
14	江西省 Jiangxi Province	赣 Gan	南昌 Nanchang
15	山东省 Shandong Province	鲁 Lu	济南 Ji'nan
16	河南省 Henan Province	豫 Yu	郑州 Zhengzhou
17	湖北省 Hubei Province	鄂 E	武汉 Wuhan
18	湖南省 Hunan Province	湘 Xiang	长沙 Changsha
19	广东省 Guangdong Province	粤 Yue	广州 Guangzhou
20	海南省 Hainan Province	琼 Qiong	海口 Haikou
21	广西壮族自治区 Guangxi Zhuang Autonomous Region	桂 Gui	南宁 Nanning
22	重庆市 Chongqing	渝 Yu	重庆 Chongqing
23	四川省 Sichuan Province	川或蜀 Chuan or Shu	成都 Chengdu
24	贵州省 Guizhou Province	贵或黔 Gui or Qian	贵阳 Guiyang
25	云南省 Yunnan Province	云或滇 Yun or Dian	昆明 Kunming
26	西藏自治区 Tibet Autonomous Region	藏 Zang	拉萨 Lhasa
27	陕西省 Shaanxi Province	陕或秦 Shaan or Qin	西安 Xi'an
28	甘肃省 Gansu Province	甘或陇 Gan or Long	兰州 Lanzhou
29	青海省 Qinghai Province	青 Qing	西宁 Xining
30	宁夏回族自治区 Ningxia Hui Autonomous Region	宁 Ning	银川 Yinchuan
31	新疆维吾尔自治区 Xinjiang Uygur Autonomous Region	新 Xin	乌鲁木齐 Urumqi
32	台湾省 Taiwan Province	台 Tai	台北 Taipei
33	香港特别行政区 Hong Kong Special Administrative Region	港 Gang	香港 Hong Kong
34	澳门特别行政区 Macao Special Administrative Region	澳 Ao	澳门 Macao

1 漠河北极村的冬天
Winter in the Arctic Village at Mohe
2 西部帕米尔高原
The Pamirs is located in the western region of China.
3. 位于南海之滨的海南岛
Hainan Island lies in the South China Sea.

中国领土的最东端是黑龙江和乌苏里江主航道中心线汇合处，最西端在新疆维吾尔自治区乌恰县西部的帕米尔高原上，东西跨经度60多度，相距5,000千米。当东海之滨的渔民迎着朝阳出海捕鱼的时候，帕米尔高原的牧民还在深夜中酣睡呢！

中国的陆地国土面积为960万平方千米，仅次于俄罗斯、加拿大，居世界第三位。另外，还拥有300万平方千米的海洋国土。

目前，中国有23个省、5个自治区、4个直辖市和两个特别行政区。首都是北京。

中国国土辽阔、资源丰富、江山多娇。中国是世界四大文明古国之一，中华民族在这块广阔的土地上，创造了光辉灿烂的东方文化。

From east to west, the territory of China extends over 60° of longitude, about 5,000 km, from the confluence of the Heilongjiang and Wusuli rivers to the Pamirs Plateau west of Wuqia County of Xinjiang Uygur Autonomous Region. When the fishermen living along the East China Sea are casting their nets in the face of the rising sun, the herdsmen on the Pamirs are still sound asleep.

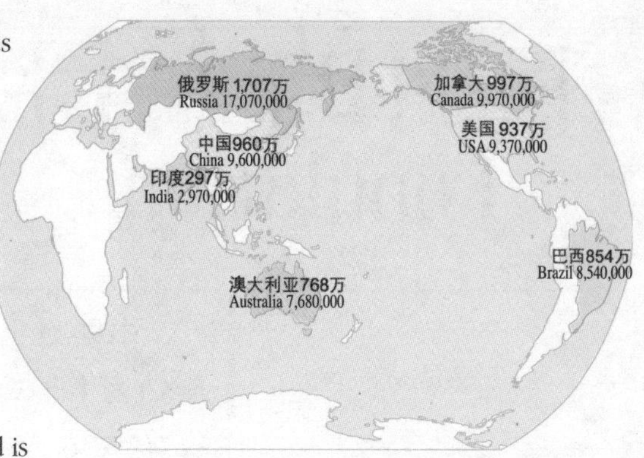

国土面积图 (单位是平方千米)
Map of Land Area (km²)

China has a land area of about 9.6 million km², and is the third largest country in the world, next only to Russia and Canada. The nation also has three million square kilometers of territorial waters.

At present, China has 23 provinces, five autonomous regions, four municipalities and two special administrative regions directly under the Central Government. The capital city is Beijing.

China has a broad territory, abundant resources and beautiful mountains and rivers. It is one of the four most ancient civilizations in the world. On this broad land Chinese people created the magnificent Eastern culture.

中国的人口
Population

中国是世界上人口数量最多的国家，截至2000年11月1日，全国总人口为12.95亿，占世界总人口的1/5左右。

China has the largest population in the world, with 1.295 billion people by the end of the 1st of November 2000, or one fifth of the world's total.

人口问题是中国面临的一个非常突出的问题。人口的过快增长给经济发展和环境保护带来了巨大的压力。20世纪70年代以来，中国政府实行了计划生育政策，大大缓解了人口压力。

人们聚集在首都北京天安门广场，庆祝国庆节

National Day celebration at Tiananmen

中国的人口，其地区分布不均匀。东部人口多，西部人口少；平原人口多，山地、高原地区人口少。

Population is a prominent problem in China, creating great pressure on economic development and environmental protection. Since the 1970s, Chinese government has pushed forward a family planning program aimed at greatly reducing this population pressure.

Moreover, the Chinese population is unevenly distributed. The east is densely populated, while the west is sparsely populated; the plains are densely populated, but the mountainous areas and plateaus are sparsely populated.

小资料 Data

2000年，中国人口的平均寿命达71.8岁。

In 2000, the average lifespan of the Chinese people reached 71.8 years.

统一的多民族大家庭
United Multi-ethnic Country

中国是一个统一的多民族国家，由汉、蒙古、回、藏、维吾尔、苗、彝、壮、布依、朝鲜、满等56个民族组成，实行民族平等的政策。在各个民族中，汉族人口最多，约占全国总人口的91.59%。除汉族以外的55个民族统称为少数民族。第五次（截至2000年11月1日）人口普查结果，少数民族总人口为10,643万，约占全国总人口的8.41%。

China is a united multi-ethnic nation of 56 ethnic groups made up of Han, Mongolian, Hui, Tibetan, Uygur, Miao, Yi, Zhuang, Bouyei, Korean, Man and so on. A policy of equity has always been promoted among the many ethnic groups. The Han ethnic group has the largest population, accounting for 91.59% of the total population. The other 55 ethnic groups are customarily referred to as national minorities. The fifth census (by the end of the 1st of November 2000) showed that the population of the ethnic groups came up to 106.43 million, accounting for about 8.41% of the total population.

1. 侗族
   Dong ethnic group
2. 哈萨克族
   Kazakh ethnic group
3. 维吾尔族
   Uygur ethnic group
4. 傈僳族
   Lisu ethnic group
5. 满族
   Manchu ethnic group

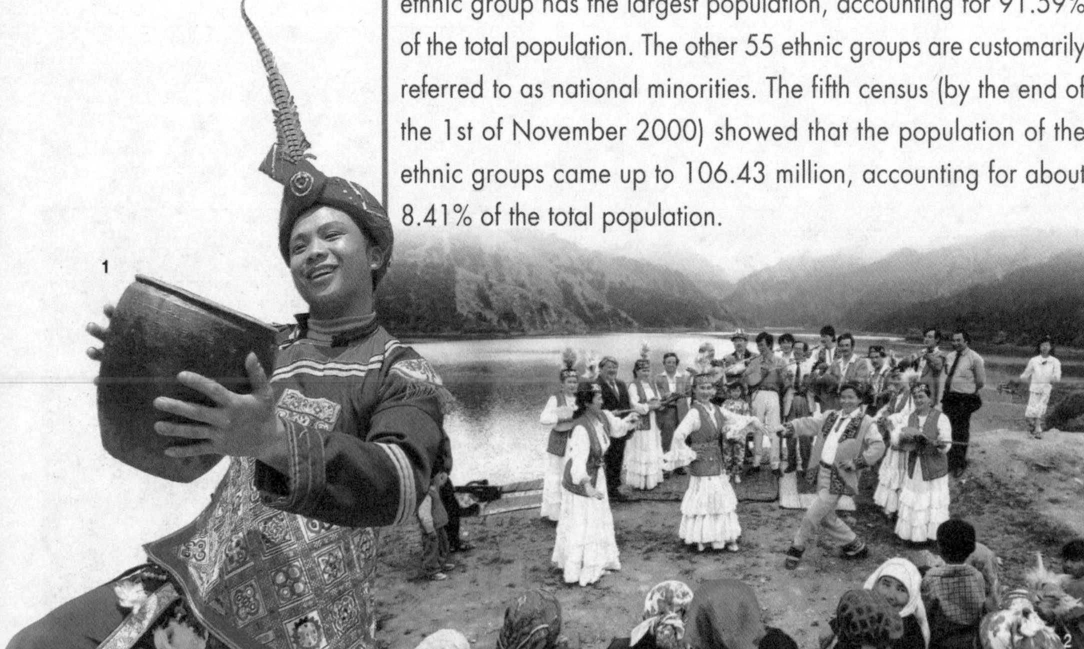
1
2

3

你知道吗 Do you know

在中国，还有一些至今未被正式识别的民族，其人数共74.9万，占全国的0.066%。

In China, there are other ethnic groups that haven't yet been formally identified, with a population of 749,000, accounting for 0.066% of the total.

少数民族人口数量虽少，但地区分布很广，主要分布在西北、西南和东北等地。维吾尔族主要分布在新疆，是一个能歌善舞的民族；蒙古族主要分布于内蒙古高原，被称为“草原民族”；藏族主要分布在青藏高原，被称为“高原之鹰”；鄂伦春族分布在兴安岭山地，被称为“山岭上人”。

千百年来，中国各族人民在不同的自然和社会历史条件下，形成了不同特色的风俗习惯。

5

The ethnic minorities, with a comparatively small population, are distributed widely in China, but are mostly congregated in the northwest, southwest and northeast. The Uygur people, good at singing and dancing, are concentrated in Xinjiang. Mongolians, long known as the “grassland people”, are mainly distributed on the Mongolian Plateau. Tibetans distributed over the Qinghai–Tibet Plateau are often called the “eagles of plateau”. The Oreqen people inhabiting the mountainous areas of the Xing'an Range are often simply called the “mountain people”.

For hundreds of years, various customs and habits of different Chinese ethnic groups have developed under different natural, social and historical conditions.

中国的地形
Topography

中国的地形复杂多样：有低平宽广的平原，有起伏和缓的丘陵，有峰峦高耸的山地，有海拔较高、面积广大的高原，有周围高、中间低的盆地。全国地势西高东低，呈三级阶梯状分布。

China's topography is very complicated. There are broad and flat plains, undulating hills, towering mountains, and vast plateaus with high altitude and dotted with basins. The terrain gradually descends from west to east like a three-step staircase.

1 阿尔泰山脉 Altai Mountains
2 准噶尔盆地 Junggar Basin
3 天山山脉 Tianshan Mountains
4 吐鲁番盆地 Turpan Basin
5 罗布泊 Lop Nor
6 内蒙古高原 Inner Mongolian Plateau
7 阴山山脉 Yinshan Mountains
8 大兴安岭 Daxing'an Mountains
9 小兴安岭 Xiaoxing'an Mountains
10 东北平原 Northeast Plain
11 长白山脉 Changbai Mountains
12 辽东丘陵 Liaodong Hills
13 塔里木河 Tarim River
14 塔里木盆地 Tarim Basin
15 帕米尔高原 The Pamirs
16 昆仑山脉 Kunlun Mountains
17 印度河 Indus River
18 青藏高原 Qinghai-Tibet Plateau
19 柴达木盆地 Qaidam Basin
20 青海湖 Qinghai Lake
21 祁连山脉 Qilian Mountains
22 黄河 Yellow River
23 六盘山 Mount Liupan
24 黄土高原 Loess Plateau
25 秦岭 Qinling Mountains
26 四川盆地 Sichuan Basin
27 巫山 Mount Wushan
28 长江中下游平原 Middle and Lower Yangtze Valley Plain
29 太行山 Taihang Mountains
30 华北平原 North China Plain
31 山东丘陵 Shandong Hills
32 朝鲜海峡 Korean Strait
33 喜马拉雅山脉 Himalayas
34 珠穆朗玛峰 Mount Qomolangma (Everest)
35 雅鲁藏布江 Yarlung Zangbo River
36 恒河 Ganges River
37 布拉马普特拉河 Brahmaputra River
38 横断山脉 Hengduan Mountains
39 云贵高原 Yunnan-Guizhou Plateau
40 雪峰山 Mount Xuefeng
41 东南丘陵 Southeast Hills
42 南岭 Nanling Mountains
43 武夷山脉 Mount Wuyi
44 洞庭湖 Dongting Lake
45 鄱阳湖 Poyang Lake
46 湄公河 Mekong River
47 马六甲海峡 Strait of Malacca

中国的气候
Climate

中国的东部是世界上典型的季风气候区，大多数地方，冬季寒冷干燥，夏季高温多雨。

The east of China is characterized by a monsoon climate. Most of the country has a cold and dry winter and hot and rainy summer.

1. 夏季，百花盛开
   Flowers blooming throughout the summer
2. 深秋，红叶满山
   The leaves turn bronze-crimson in autumn.

中国一月平均气温
Average Temperature in January in China

中国七月平均气温
Average Temperature in July in China

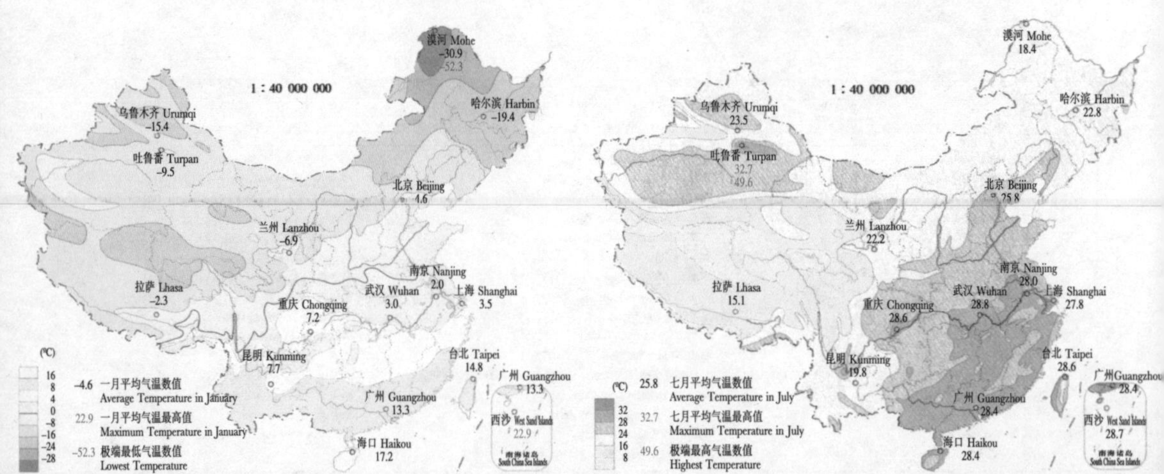

中国年降水量
Average Annual Precipitation in China

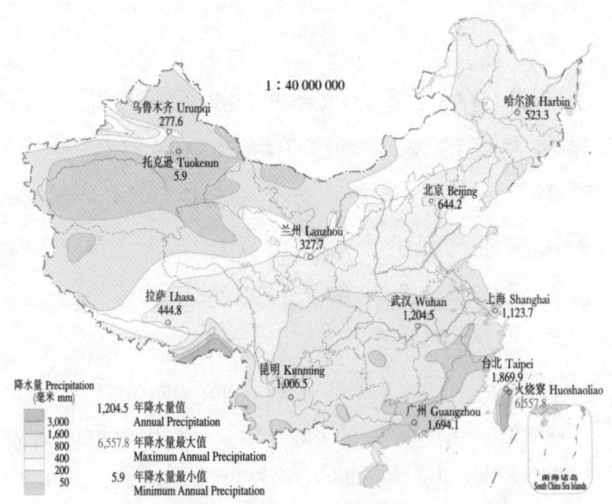

冬季，南北的气温差别较大，当北方的哈尔滨人冒着严寒参观“冰灯游园会”时，南方的广州却是百花盛开，春意盎然。

夏季，全国大部分地区普遍炎热，降水较多，雨热同季，给农业带来了极大好处。

全国的降水量，地区分布不均匀。东南部地区较多，台湾省的火烧寮，年平均降水量多达6,557.8毫米；西北部地区降水少，新疆吐鲁番盆地中部，年平均降水量不到10毫米。

In winter, there is a big temperature difference between north and south. When people of Harbin brave the deep snow to visit the annual “Ice Lantern Garden Party”, people in Guangzhou are enjoying a beautiful spring with flowers in bloom. In summer, most of China is very hot with plentiful rainfall, greatly benefiting agriculture.

Precipitation is unevenly distributed, resulting in plentiful rain in the southeast but little in the northwest. In Huoshaoliao of Taiwan, the average annual precipitation reaches 6,557.8 mm, while in the middle of the Turpan Basin in Xinjiang it drops to below 10 mm.

你知道吗 Do you know

“季风”可以简单地理解为风向随季节而发生显著变化的风。中国东部夏季盛行东南风，冬季盛行西北风。

Monsoon is when the wind direction changes distinctively with the seasons. In summer, the east of China enjoys a southeastern monsoon, and in winter a northwestern monsoon.

每年的6～7月，江淮地区阴雨连绵，此时正是梅子成熟的季节，所以人们称这种雨为“梅雨”。由于这一时期多雨阴湿，物品容易霉烂，又俗称“霉雨”。

From June to July every year, it is overcast and rainy in the drainage areas of the Yangtze and Huaihe rivers when the red bayberry ripens. Therefore, people also call the rain of this period “red bayberry rain”. And, because things easily go moldy in this period, the rain is also called “moldy rain”.

小资料 Data

北京与纽约的纬度位置相近，但是，北京冬季比纽约冷，夏季比纽约热。7月份与1月份的气温相比，北京相差30.9℃，纽约相差23.6℃。

Beijing and New York are almost at the same latitude. But Beijing's winter is colder than New York's, while its summer is hotter. Between July and January, there is an average temperature difference of 30.9°C in Beijing, while in New York it is only 23.6°C.

中国的经济
Economy

中国自1978年实行改革开放的政策以来，经济获得了持续快速的发展。目前经济总量已位居世界前列。其中，粮食、棉花、肉类、布匹、钢、原煤、电视机等工农业产品的产量尤为突出；原子能、生物技术、计算机技术、航空航天技术等方面也已经达到或接近世界先进水平。

Since China launched its reform and opening up policy in 1978, the economy has been developing at a continuously high rate. The industrial and agricultural products of grain, cotton, meat, cloth, steel, raw coal and TV sets have grown markedly; and the technologies of atomic energy, biology, computers, aviation and aerospace and so on have reached the world level.

1978~1999年中国国民生产总值

China's GNP 1978~1999

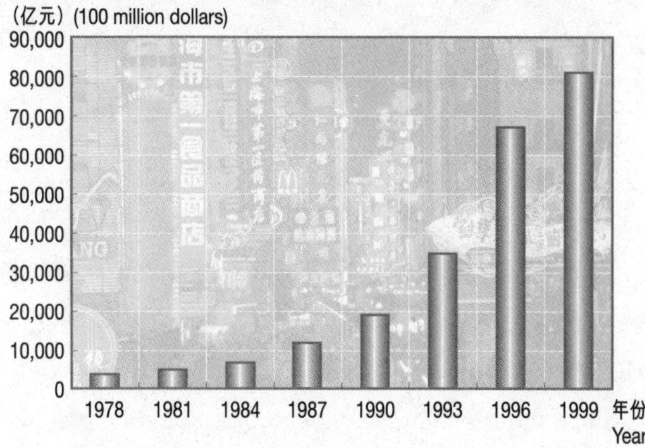

中国改革开放以后，从海外引进了大量的人才、资金和技术，大大加快了经济发展的步伐。预计到21世纪中叶，中国将基本上实现现代化，达到中等发达国家的水平。

中国是一个人口大国，按人口平均的经济水平还不高，仍然属于低收入国家，与发达国家相比，还存在较大的差距。中国经济发展水平的地区差异较大，东部沿海地区比较发达，而西部地区相对落后。中国正在进行西部大开发，以加快西部地区经济发展的步伐。

1. 北京王府井商业街
Wangfujing Commercial Street, Beijing
2. 上海集装箱码头
Shanghai Container Terminal

Since the reform and opening up, China has introduced a lot of talented personnel, capital and technologies from other countries, greatly accelerating economic growth. It is estimated that by the middle of the 21st century, China will be generally modernized and reached the level of the middle-developed countries.

China is a country with a large population. Calculated according to per capita income, the economic level is still low, and there still exists a fairly large gap with the developed countries. China's economic level varies according to region. The areas along the coast in eastern China are rather developed, while those in the west are backward. China is carrying out a western development plan to promote rapid economic growth in that region.

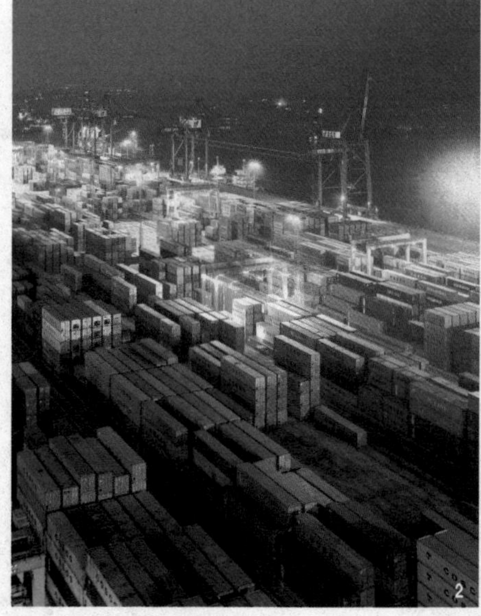
2

中国的工业
Industry

1949年中华人民共和国成立以后，工业发展迅速，现在已建立了独立完整的现代化工业体系，拥有钢铁、化工、机械、纺织、电子、航空航天等所有的工业门类。

Since the founding of the People's Republic of China in 1949, industry has been developing fast so that an independent and complete modern industrial system has now been established. All industrial categories are represented, such as iron, chemicals, machine building, textile, electronics, aviation and aerospace and so on.

1

1. 新疆独山子炼油厂
A petroleum refinery company at Dushanzi, Xinjiang
2. 乌鲁木齐石化总厂
Urumqi Petrochemical Company
3. 鞍山钢铁厂
Anshan's Iron and Steel Works
4. 四川西昌备用的长城火箭
The Great Wall Rocket is kept in Xichang, Sichuan Province.

1949年以前，中国的工业大部分都分布在沈阳、大连、天津、青岛、上海、广州等东部沿海城市，广大的中、西部地区，除武汉、重庆等少数城市外，工业水平都非常低。

1949年以后，中国工业的地区分布发生了很大的变化，已形成了辽宁省中、南部地区的重工业基地；以北京—天津—唐山为中心的综合性工业基地；以上海—南京—杭州为中心的全国最大的综合性工业基地；珠江三角洲地区以广州、深圳为主的综合性工业基地。

Before 1949, most Chinese industrial enterprises were distributed in Shenyang, Dalian, Tianjin, Qingdao, Shanghai and Guangzhou along the east coast. The large areas in the middle and west of China, excluding Wuhan, Chongqing, etc., had fewer industries by comparison.

Since 1949, great changes have taken place in the distribution of industry, forming a heavy industrial base in the middle and south of Liaoning Province; a comprehensive industrial base focusing on Beijing, Tianjin and Tangshan; the largest comprehensive industrial base focusing on Shanghai, Nanjing and Hangzhou; and a comprehensive industrial base centered on Guangzhou and Shenzhen in the Pearl River Delta.

你知道吗 Do you know

中国是世界上最大的电视机、钢、水泥、原煤、化肥生产国。

China is the largest producer of TV sets, steel, cement, raw coal and fertilizer in the world.

中国的农业
Agriculture

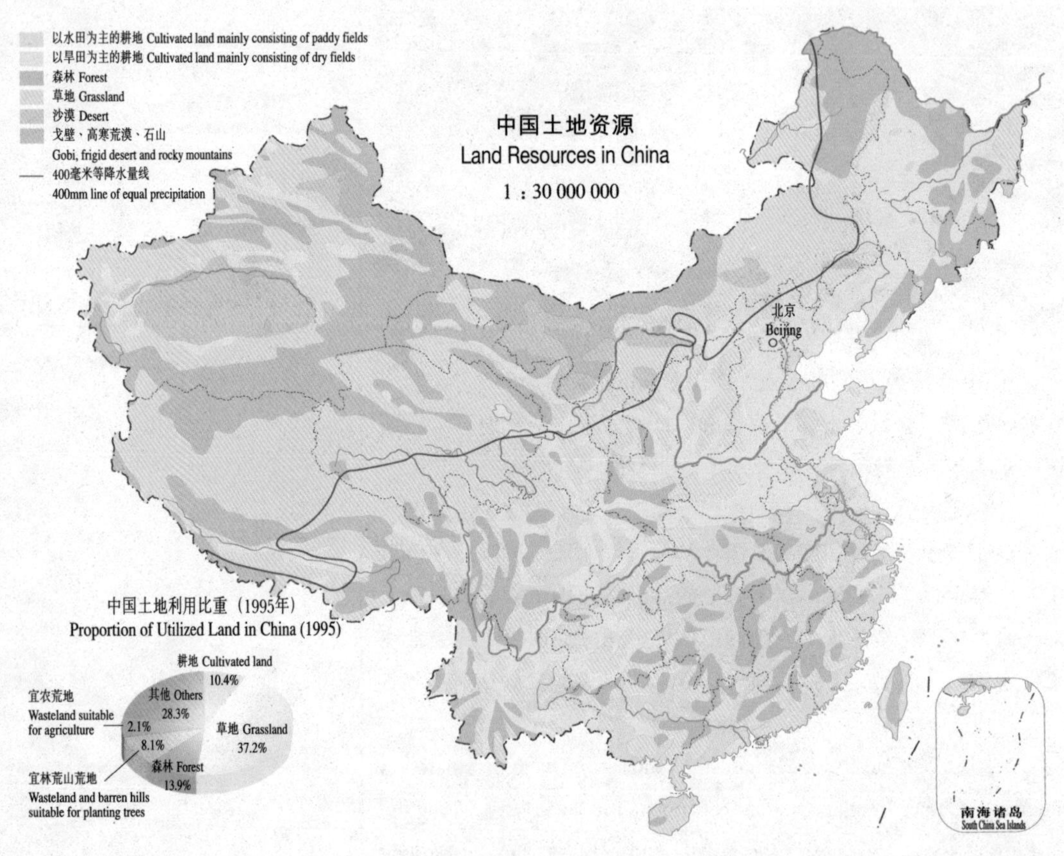

中国是一个农业大国，同时也是世界上农业发展历史最悠久的国家之一，水稻等主要农作物都起源于中国。

China is a big agricultural country with one of the longest histories of agricultural development. Crops such as rice originated in China.

中国政府十分重视农业生产，不断加大农业投入，积极进行农田水利基本建设，从而提高了农业生产的现代化水平，使农业取得了辉煌的成就。最突出的表现是：中国仅依靠占世界不足10%的耕地，养活了占世界1/5以上的人口。

1978~1999 年中国主要农产品产量图

Output of China's Major Agricultural Products 1978~1999

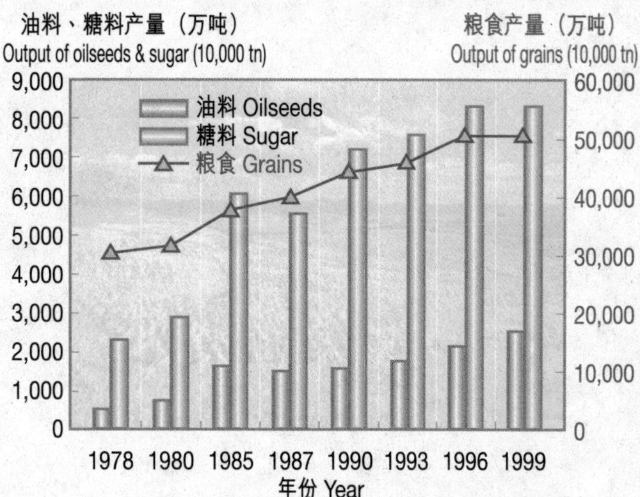

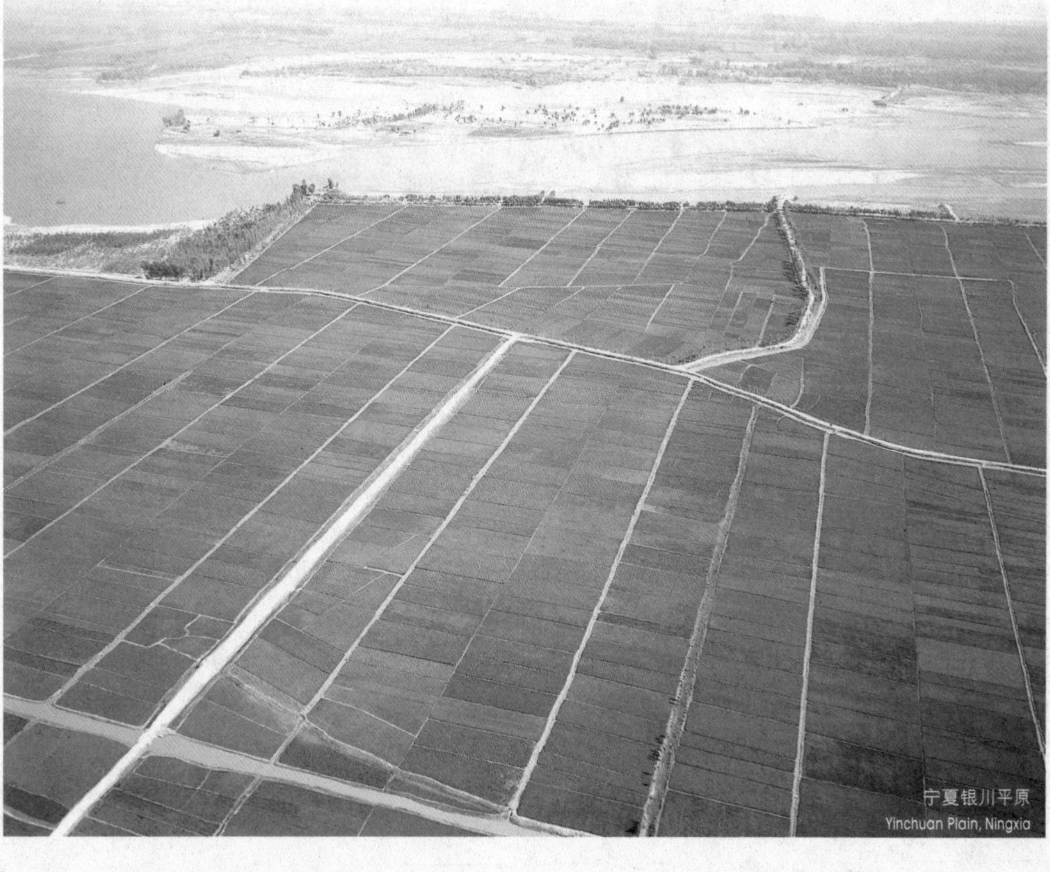

宁夏银川平原

Yinchuan Plain, Ningxia

黑龙江农村，农民用收割机收麦
Harvesting machines are widely used by farmers in Heilongjiang.

你知道吗 Do you know

中国各种农产品的产量增长很快，谷物、肉类、棉花、油菜、花生、水果的总产量均居世界第一位。但是，由于人口数量多，人均占有的农产品数量较少。

China's output of various agricultural products has a fast growth rate. The total output of grains, meat, cotton, rape, peanuts and fruits tops the world. However, due to the large population, the amount of the agricultural products per capita is small.

The Chinese government has been paying close attention to agriculture, increasing investment and actively carrying out irrigation and water conservancy capital construction to speed up the modernization of agricultural production. This has led to great achievements, the most outstanding being that, with less than ten percent of the world's cultivatable land, China manages to feed over one-fifth of the world's population.

锦绣河山 Land of Charm and Beauty

喜马拉雅山
The Himalayas

喜马拉雅山脉位于青藏高原的南缘，西起帕米尔高原，东到雅鲁藏布江大拐弯处，东西长2,450千米，南北宽200～300千米，平均海拔6,200米。

The Himalayas, bordered by the Qinghai-Tibet Plateau to the north, extend from the Pamirs in the west to the great turning point of the Yarlung Zangbo River in the east. From east to west, and from south to north, the mountains span over 2,450 km and 200—300 km, respectively, with an average altitude of 6,200 m.

1

喜马拉雅山脉海拔7,000米以上的高峰有40座。主峰珠穆朗玛峰海拔8,848.13米，是世界第一高峰，位于中国与尼泊尔的边界上，如同一座美丽的金字塔雄踞在喜马拉雅山的中段。

喜马拉雅山是地球上最年轻的山脉，因为它真正成为雄伟的山体仅有几十万年的历史，而且现在还在不断增高呢！

The Himalayas comprise 40 mountains which are over 7,000 m high. Qomolangma (Mt. Everest) is the highest mountain in the world, with an altitude of 8,848.13 m. Located on the border of China and Nepal, it dominates the middle of the Himalayas like a majestic pyramid.

The Himalayas are the youngest mountains on earth because they only emerged several hundred thousand years from the sea after great subterranean upheavals. Hence, they are still growing!

你知道吗 Do you know

藏语中"喜马拉雅"是"冰雪之乡"的意思。7,000米以上的高峰，山顶终年被积雪覆盖，冰川广布。

"Himalayas" in the Tibetan language means "land of snow". The mountains over 7,000 m are snow-capped all year round and glaciers can be found everywhere.

1. 喜马拉雅山的山顶终年被积雪覆盖
The peaks of Himalayas are covered with snow all year round.
2. 珠穆朗玛峰
Qomolangma (Mt. Everest)

秦 岭
The Qinling Mountains

秦岭的最高峰是太白山，海拔3,767米。另一高峰华山海拔虽不过2,000多米，但山势险要，有"自古华山一条路"和"奇险天下第一山"之说。巨大的花岗岩体组成的五个峻峭山峰(东峰、西峰、南峰、北峰和中峰)，像一朵五瓣的梅花绽开在山顶上，景色奇丽。

Taibai Peak is the highest peak of the Qinling Mountains, with an altitude of 3,767 m. Mount Hua, though only about 2,000 m high, is precipitous, resulting in the expressions, "there is one access to Mount Hua since ancient times" and "the first precipitous mountain under heaven". The five peaks, namely the East Peak, West Peak, South Peak, North Peak and Middle Peak, stand like a five-petal plum flower in full blossom. Mount Hua has unique and charming scenery.

1

秦岭好像一堵挡风的高墙，横卧在中国的腹部。冬季，它阻挡着南下凛冽的西北风，使南方受寒潮影响减弱；夏季，它阻截了东南风带来的水气，使北方降水大为减少。因此，秦岭是中国南北之间一条重要的地理分界线。

The Qinling Mountains stand like a huge wall blocking the wind in the hinterland of China. In winter, they stop the northwest wind from blowing southward, reducing the cold wave influence on the south of China; in summer, they intercept the vapor brought by the southeast wind, reducing precipitation in North China. Therefore, these mountains play a very important geographical role in acting as a dividing line between the south and north of China.

1. 秦岭太白山景色
Scenery of the Qinling Mountains
2. 华山
Mount Hua

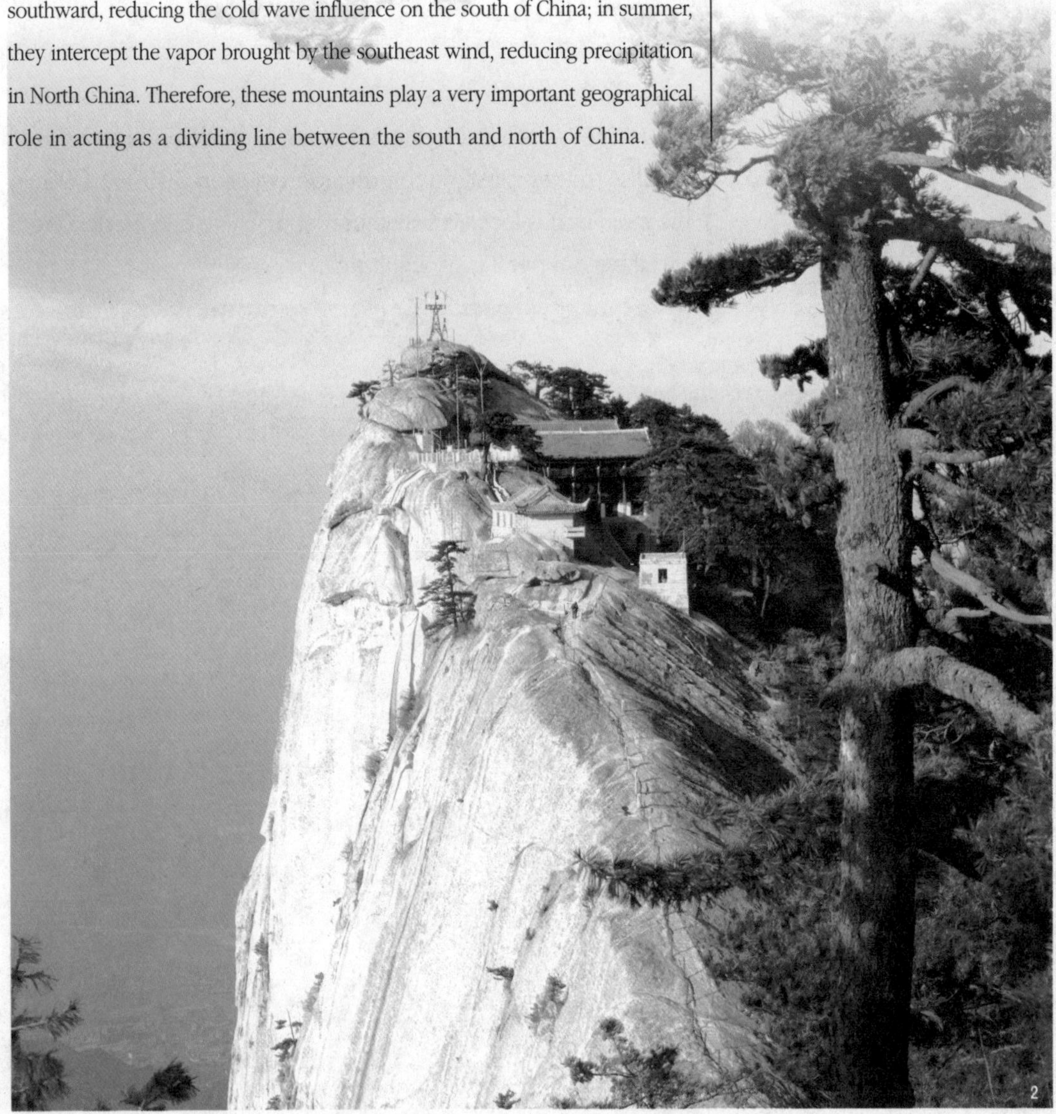
2

长白山
The Changbai Mountains

长白山是东北东部山地的总称，由一系列平行排列的山岭组成，海拔多在500～1,000米，主体部分位于中朝边境，主峰是白头山。

Changbai Mountains, the general term for the eastern mountainous area in Northeast China, is made up of a series of parallel ranges mostly at an altitude between 500 – 1,000 m. The main part is located on the border of China and North Korea, and the main peak is Mount Baitou.

2

3

4

5

白头山天池

白头山天池位于白头山山顶，它是因火山口积水而形成的湖泊，池水清澈如镜，周围被峭壁山峰环绕，湖山相映，景色优美。

长白山是一座自然资源的大宝库。从山脚到峰顶气候变化万千，景色十分壮观。人们经常提到的"东北三宝"——人参、貂皮、鹿茸就产于此地。

The Heavenly Pond of Mount Baitou

The Heavenly Pond of Mount Baitou lies on the top of Mount Baitou, and is a lake formed by water accumulated in the crater. Its reflection is as clear as a mirror. Encircled by precipitous mountains, the pond sets the mountains off, forming beautiful scenery.

The Changbai Mountains are a great treasure house of natural resources. The "three treasures of the Northeast" often mentioned by people—ginseng, mink and pilose antler—are produced here.

1. 白头山天池
   Heavenly Pond on Mount Baitou
2. 长白山主峰白头山
   The Main Peak of Changbai Mountains — Mount Baitou
3. 紫貂
   Sable
4. 鹿茸
   Pilose antlers
5. 人参
   Ginseng

天山
The Tianshan Mountains

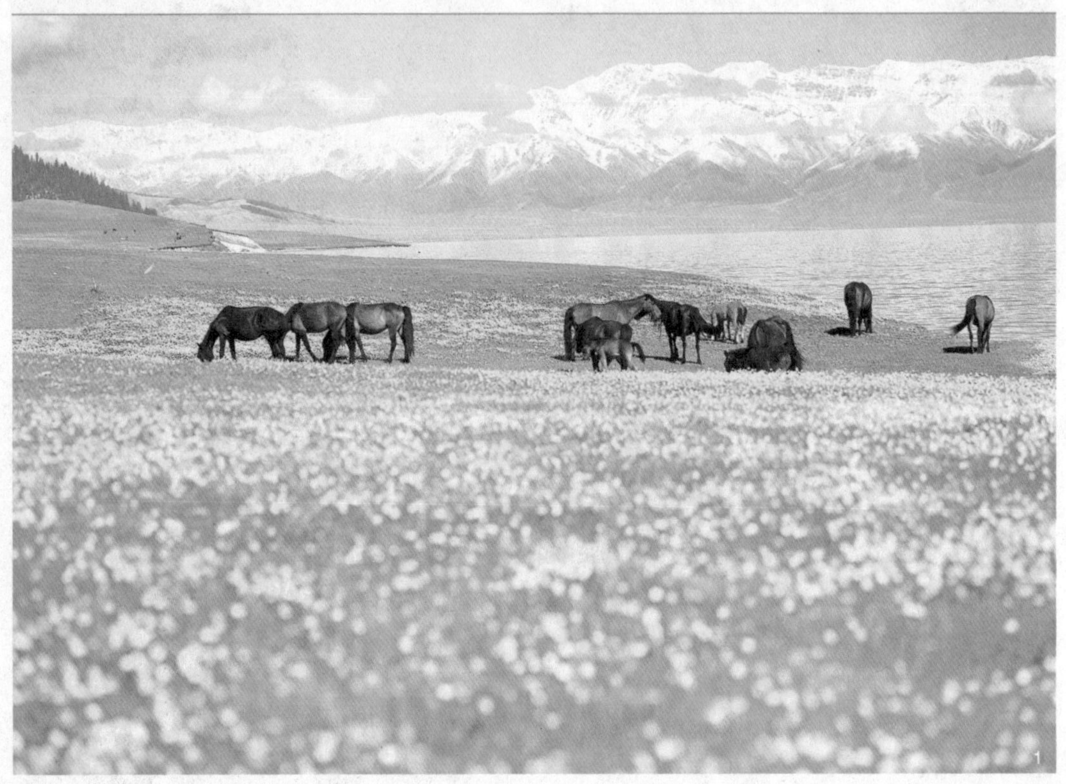

天山山脉全长2,500千米，分为西天山、中天山和东天山三部分。西天山在哈萨克斯坦境内，东天山和中天山横贯中国新疆中部。

The Tianshan Mountains, with a total length of 2,500 km, includes the Western Tianshan Mountain, the Middle Tianshan Mountain and the Eastern Tianshan Mountain. The Western Tianshan Mountain is located in the territory of Kazakhstan. The Eastern Tianshan Mountain and the Middle Tianshan Mountain cross the middle of Xinjiang in China.

天山景色秀丽。举目远望，只见山顶上白雪皑皑，冰川蜿蜒；山腰森林片片，绿草如茵；山脚下流水淙淙，一块块绿洲如花似锦。雄伟壮丽的天山是新疆维吾尔自治区重要的牧业生产基地之一。

These mountains offer graceful scenery. Seen from afar, they are snow-capped and covered by glaciers with green trees and grass thriving up to the midway point. At the foot of the mountain, tinkling streams and oases provide a picturesque touch. The area is one of the bases of animal husbandry of the Xinjiang Uygur Autonomous Region.

2

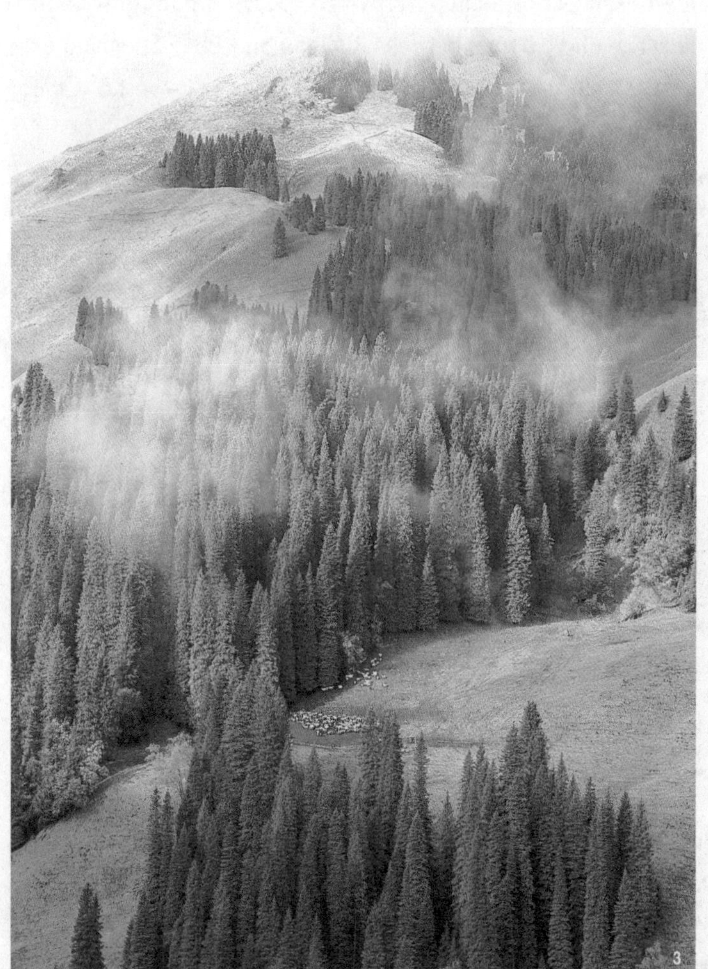

3

1. 天山夏季牧场
   The Tianshan Mountains' pasture during summer time
2. 天山雪景
   Snow-capped Tianshan Mountains
3. 天山西部巩乃斯原始森林
   Gongnaisi virgin forest, western Tianshan

昆仑山
The Kunlun Mountains

昆仑山西起帕米尔高原，东经青海省到四川省西北部，横贯新疆和西藏之间，全长2,500千米，它像一条长龙横卧在中国的西部，有“亚洲脊柱”之称。

The Kunlun Mountains extend from the Pamirs in the west to the northwest of Sichuan Province, passing through Qinghai Province and crossing between Xinjiang and Tibet. Spanning over 2,500 km, they crouch like a long dragon in the west of China, and are called the "spine of Asia".

1

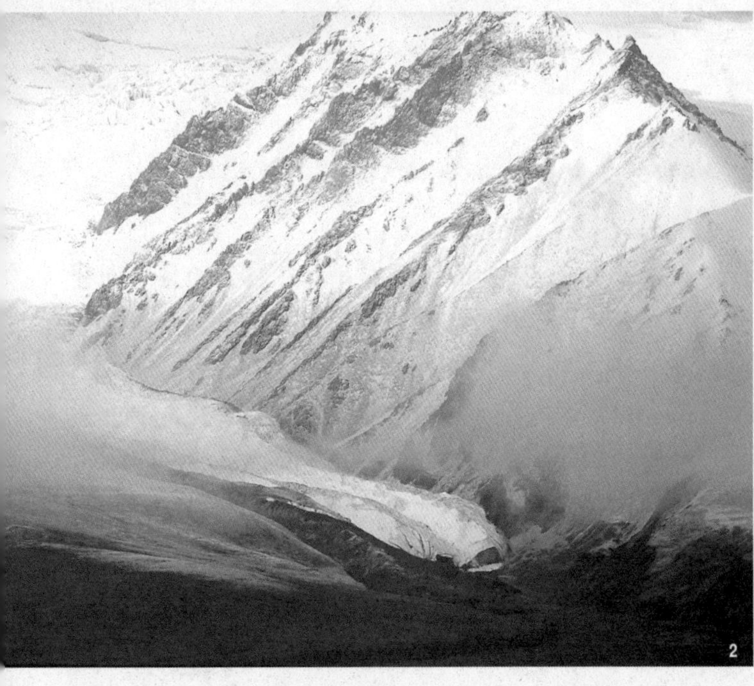

1. 巍巍昆仑山
The Kunlun Mountains
2. 昆仑山玉柱山
Mount Yuzhu of the Kunlun Mountains

昆仑山由东、中、西昆仑三部分组成。东昆仑像一只鸟爪一样分出南、中、北三支脉，属于南支的巴颜喀拉山是长江和黄河的分水岭。

昆仑山海拔多在5,000米以上，许多高峰超过7,000米。每年夏天山顶积雪开始融化，汇成一股股清澈的溪流，滋润着西北干旱的土地，补充着长江和黄河的水源。

The Kunlun Mountains comprise the Eastern, Middle and Western Kunlun Mountains. The southern, middle and northern branch ranges of Eastern Kunlun Mountains spread like a claw of a bird. The Bayakala Mountain, belonging to the southern branch, is the watershed of the Yangtze and Yellow rivers.

Most of the peaks in the Kunlun range are over 5,000 m above sea level, and some of them reach more than 7,000 m. Every summer, snow on the top of the mountains begins to melt, forming streams which moisten the dry land in Northwest and supplement the sources of the Yangtze and Yellow rivers.

小资料 Data

昆仑山气候严寒，冰峰雪岭连绵不断，是中国冰川最多的山，高峰慕士塔格山有“冰川之父”的称号。众多的冰川如条条玉龙盘旋于山谷中，冰塔林、冰瀑布、冰裂缝琳琅满目。丰富的冰川与积雪，成为许多江河的源泉。

The Kunlun Mountains with undulating ice-capped peaks have freezing weather and the most glaciers in China. The Muztag Ata Mountain is reputed to be "the father of glaciers". Numerous glaciers are entrenched in valleys like jade dragons. Seracs, icy waterfalls and ice cracks can be found everywhere. A lot of glaciers and accumulated snow become the sources of many rivers.

青藏高原
The Qinghai-Tibet Plateau

青藏高原位于中国西南部，面积约230万平方千米，平均海拔4,000米以上，被称为“世界屋脊”，是中国的第一大高原。

Located in the southwest of China, the Qinghai-Tibet Plateau has an area of about 2.3 million km^2 and an average altitude of over 4,000 m. It is honored as the "roof of the world" and is the biggest plateau in China.

1

青藏高原是典型的山地型高原。主要有阿尔金山、祁连山、昆仑山、喀喇昆仑山、唐古拉山、冈底斯山、念青唐古拉山、横断山脉以及喜马拉雅山等高大山脉。世界最高峰——珠穆朗玛峰就是喜马拉雅山的主峰。

青藏高原气温低，雪山连绵，形成了大面积的高山冰川，被称为“固体水库”。冰雪融水不仅是亚洲许多著名大河的源流，也是中国内陆干旱地区重要的灌溉水源。

青藏高原是中国重要的天然牧场，高原上的草并不高，但因光照充足，光合作用旺盛，营养价值极高。每年夏秋季节，草原上牛羊成群，除了放牧的牦牛、藏山羊、藏绵羊和犏牛外，还有成群的黄羊、羚羊、野牛、野驴等野生动物。

1. 鸟瞰冈底斯山
The bird's-eye view of Gandise Mountains
2. 高原之舟——牦牛
Ships of the Plateau — Yaks

The Qinghai-Tibet Plateau is a typical mountainous plateau. It mainly comprises Altyn Tagh Mountains, Qilian Mountains, Kunlun Mountains, Karakorum Mountains, Tanggula Mountains, Gandise Mountains, Nyaindqentanglha Mountains, Hengduan Mountains and the Himalayas. Qomolangma (Mt. Everest)—the highest mountain in the world—is the main peak of the Himalayas.

The Qinghai-Tibet Plateau has low temperature, undulating snow-capped mountains and a large area of glaciers, so it is called a "solid water reservoir". The melted ice and snow is not only the source of many famous rivers in Asia, but also the irrigating source of the inland dry areas in China.

The plateau is an important natural pasture in China. The grasses growing there is not tall, but because of the rich sunshine and active photosynthesis, they are very nutritious. Every summer and fall, herds of cows and sheep graze there. Apart from grazing yaks, Tibetan goats, Tibetan sheep and *pian niu* (offspring of a bull and a female yak), there are herds of Mongolian gazelle, antelopes, wild ox, Asiatic wild ass, and many other wild animals.

小资料 Data

青藏高原是中国湖泊最稠密的地区之一，湖泊总面积有3万多平方千米，约占全国的40％。全国面积最大的咸水湖——青海湖就在青藏高原上。

The Qinghai-Tibet Plateau is one of the areas with the densest distribution of lakes. The total area of the lakes on the plateau is more than 30,000 km^2, accounting for 40% of the total in China. Qinghai Lake, the largest salt lake in China, also lies on the plateau.

内蒙古高原
The Inner Mongolian Plateau

内蒙古高原位于中国北部，面积约100万平方千米，平均海拔1,000米以上，是中国的第二大高原。

With an area of about one million square kilometers and an altitude of more than 1,000 m, the Inner Mongolian Plateau is located in the north of China and is the second largest plateau in the country.

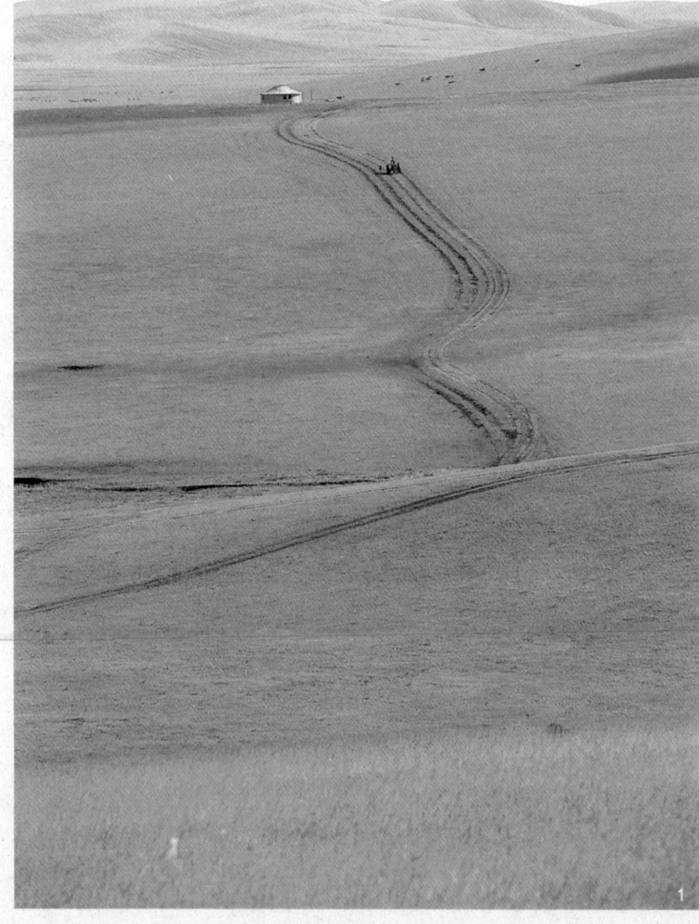

1. 内蒙古呼伦贝尔草原
   Hulunbeier Grasslands of Inner Mongolia
2. 内蒙坝上
   The flat land of Inner Mongolia
3. 腾格里大沙漠
   The Tengger Desert
4. 内蒙古高原是著名的天然草场
   The Inner Mongolian Plateau is the famous natural grassland in China.

内蒙古高原开阔坦荡，地面起伏和缓。从飞机上俯视高原就像烟波浩瀚的大海。

2

高原上既有碧野千里的草原，也有沙浪滚滚的沙漠，是中国天然牧场和沙漠分布地区之一。

内蒙古高原气候十分干燥，沙漠分布面积占全国沙漠总面积的1/3以上。较大的沙漠有巴丹吉林沙漠、腾格里沙漠、乌兰布和沙漠和库布齐沙漠等。

3

黄河流经内蒙古高原中部时，河谷较宽展，泥沙在此堆积，成为肥沃的冲积平原，这就是被人们称为"塞上江南"的河套平原。

内蒙古高原是中国著名的天然草场。"天苍苍，野茫茫，风吹草低见牛羊"，曾是对草原的真实写照。但由于过度放牧等原因，导致草场退化，出现了荒漠化的现象。所以，中国正在实施的西部大开发战略，把改善生态环境作为重要举措之一。

4

The Inner Mongolian Plateau is vast, with a moderately undulating surface. Seen from a plane, it looks like an immense sea. The plateau has not only vast green pastures, but also deserts of billowing sand. It is one of the areas where natural pasture and desert are distributed.

The Inner Mongolian Plateau has very dry weather and more than one–third of the total desert in China. There are comparatively big deserts, such as the Badain Jaran Desert, Tengger Desert, Ulanbu Desert and Kubuqi Desert.

The Yellow River passes through the Inner Mongolian Plateau, where the river valley expands and sand accumulates into the Hetao Plain—a fertile alluvial plain—which is called "Jiangnan (areas south of the lower reaches of the Yangtze River) beyond the Great Wall" by people.

The Inner Mongolian Plateau is the famous natural grassland in China. The verse of "under boundless sky, on vast plains, cows and sheep can be seen when the wind blows and grass lowers" draws a vivid picture of the region. Due to the excessive grazing, the grassland has degenerated into desert in many places. Therefore, environmental improvement is an important part of the government's western region development strategy.

黄土高原
The Loess Plateau

1. 千沟万壑的黄土高原
Bizarre geomorphology on the Loess Plateau
2. 黄土高原的窑洞和民族风情，吸引着各地游客
The cave dwellings and the folk customs of the Loess Plateau attract tourists from worldwide.
3. 黄土高原地面覆盖着厚厚的黄土
The Loess Plateau is covered by a thick layer of loess.

黄土高原面积约40万平方千米，是中国的第三大高原，平均海拔在1,000～2,000米，绝大部分的地面覆盖着50～80米厚的黄土。

在如此大的面积之上，覆盖着这么厚的黄土，是世界上任何地区都无法比拟的，是大自然创造的一个奇迹。

With an area of about 400,000 km^2 and an average altitude of between 1,000 – 2,000 m, the Loess Plateau is the third largest plateau in China and is mostly covered by a 50 – 80 m-thick layer of loess, which is incomparable in the world and a miracle of nature.

1

2

3

黄土地貌

黄土高原，千沟万壑。壮观的土柱、奇特的峰丛，以及窑洞和民族风情，都吸引着各地的游客。

黄土高原的水土流失非常严重，大量的黄土被雨水冲刷到黄河里，使黄河水中含有大量的泥沙，也使高原表面形成许多沟谷。科学家们的研究结果告诉我们，黄土本身质地疏松，对流水侵蚀的抵抗力极弱，而黄土高原的降水又多为暴雨，侵蚀力非常强。加上不合理的土地利用，滥垦滥伐等人为因素的破坏，更加剧了水土流失。目前，中国政府正通过退耕还林、退耕还草等措施来治理黄土高原上的水土流失。

Geomorphology of Loess

The Loess Plateau has millions of gullies. The splendid loess pillars, peculiar peaks, cave dwellings and folk customs attract tourists from everywhere.

But the plateau has suffered from a serious loss of water and land erosion. Much of the loess is flushed away into the Yellow River by rain, filling it with mud and sand and carving out many gullies as it is carried away towards the sea. Research shows that exposed to thunderstorms, the porous loess can hardly avoid becoming eroded by the flowing water. This has been exacerbated by man-made devastation such as unreasonable land utilization and excessive deforestation. Now, the Chinese government is taking measures for reforesting some of the cultivated land and planting grass to control the loss of water and erosion.

你知道吗 Do you know

黄土形成于干旱或半干旱的大陆性气候条件下，其物质来源于高原西北部遥远的中亚、蒙古的戈壁和荒漠。干燥、强劲的西北风源源不断地把那些风化形成的细小物质带到东南面来，沿途逐渐堆积下来，年深日久，就形成了黄土高原。

Loess is engendered under the conditions of a dry or semi-dry continental climate. The matter of the loess comes from the faraway Central Asia, the Mongolian Gobi and deserts to the northwest of the plateau. The dry and strong northwest wind keeps bringing the efflorescent particles to the southeast. Those particles are deposited year by year, thus forming the Loess Plateau.

云贵高原
The Yunnan-Guizhou Plateau

云贵高原主要分布在云南、贵州省境内，面积约40万平方千米，平均海拔1,000～2,000米，是中国的第四大高原。

With an area of about 400,000 km^2 and an average altitude of 1,000 – 2,000 m, the Yunnan-Guizhou Plateau is located in Yunnan and Guizhou provinces and is the fourth largest plateau in China.

众多的河流穿插在云贵高原上，不停地切割着地面，形成许多又深又陡的峡谷。云贵高原西高东低。云南境内的高原地形相对完整，多山间小盆地；贵州境内的高原地形支离破碎，崎岖不平，人们常用“地无三里平”来形容这种状况。

盆地内土层深厚而肥沃，是农业比较发达的地方，高原上的城镇也都集中在这里。

云贵高原分布着广泛的喀斯特地貌，它是石灰岩在高温多雨的条件下，经过漫长的岁月，被水溶解和侵蚀而逐渐形成的。地下和地表分布着许多溶洞、暗河、石芽、石笋、峰林等稀奇古怪的地貌。云贵高原是世界上喀斯特地貌发育最完美、最典型的地区之一。

A great number of rivers have scoured many deep and steep valleys on the Yunnan-Guizhou Plateau as it descends from west to east. The terrain in Yunnan Province, where there are many basins among the mountains, is comparatively complete, while that of the plateau in Guizhou Province is bumpy and irregular, causing people to say that, “there is no flat ground within three *li* (Chinese unit of length——half a kilometer)”.

The basins have deep and fertile soil where agriculture is well developed and towns are concentrated.

Karst topography is widely distributed on the Yunnan-Guizhou Plateau. Karst forms gradually after limestone is dissolved and eroded by water over a long period of time under the conditions of high temperature and plentiful rain. There are many caves, underground rivers, stone roots, stalagmites and other odd topography. The Yunnan-Guizhou Plateau is one of the areas where the Karst topography has developed most completely and typically in the world.

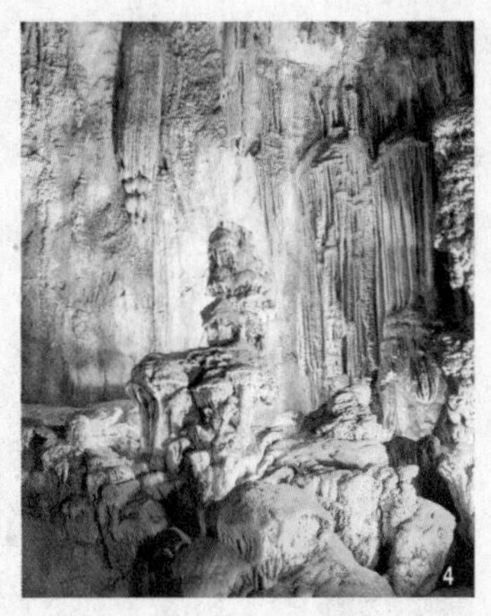

4

小知识 Knowledge

当地人把小盆地叫“坝子”，大的坝子面积可达50平方千米以上，小的只有1平方千米左右。

The local people call basins *bazi* in Chinese. Big basins can cover more than 50 km², but the small ones are only about one square kilometer.

2

3

1. 云贵高原上的梯田
   Terraced fields on the Yunnan-Guizhou Plateau
2. 山间小盆地——“坝子”
   A basin — *bazi* — surrounded by mountains
3. 云南红土地
   The laterite landscape of Yunnan
4. 地下溶洞
   Underground cave

东北平原
The Northeast Plain

东北平原山环水绕、沃野千里，面积约35万平方千米，是中国的第一大平原。

The Northeast Plain surrounded by mountains and rivers has boundless fertile fields. With an area of about 350,000 km^2, it is the biggest plain in China.

东北平原以黑土著称。黑土含有大量的有机质，人们形容它“用手一捏直冒油，插根柴禾也发芽”。东北平原是中国最重要的粮食产地。

东北平原地下蕴藏着石油、煤炭等丰富的矿产资源。著名的大庆油田就位于它的北部。

The Northeast Plain is famous for its black soil, which contains a lot of organic substances. People describe it in such words as “oil will leak out if you nip the soil; even a branch can bud in it”.

The Northeast Plain is the most important grain producing area in China, but it also contains oil, coal and other mineral resources. The famous Daqing Oilfield is located in the north of the plain.

小资料 Data

东北平原由三江平原、松嫩平原和辽河平原三部分组成。

The Northeast Plain is composed of the Sanjiang Plain, Songnen Plain and Liaohe Plain.

1. 东北平原是中国最重要的粮食产地
The Northeast Plain accounts for the majority of China's agricultural production.
2. 黑龙江的农田
The farmland of Heilongjiang
3. 东北平原的优质黑土地
Rich black soil on the Northeast Plain

华北平原
The North China Plain

华北平原地势平坦，一望无际，面积约31万平方千米，是中国的第二大平原。

The North China Plain, flat and vast, is the second largest one in China. It has an area of about 310,000 km^2.

1

过去，华北平原许多地方经常发生旱涝灾害，有“大雨大灾，小雨小灾，无雨旱灾”之说。

近几十年来，中国政府大力发展水利事业，初步建成了一套完整的排水防旱系统，极大地改变了本地区多灾多难的面貌。如今，这里已成为著名的粮食和棉花产地。

华北平原范围大，人口多，资源丰富，经济比较发达。北京、天津、济南、徐州等重要城市均分布在此。

In the past, many places in the North China Plain suffered from floods and drought. There was a saying that a "big disaster is when it is raining hard, a small disaster is when it is drizzling, and drought comes when there is no rain".

In recent decades, the Chinese government has been developing water conservancy projects and has built up a comprehensive system of drainage for dealing with floods and averting droughts. Now, the area has become a famous grain and cotton producing area.

The North China Plain has a large area and population, rich resources and fairly well developed economy. Some important cities like Beijing, Tianjin, Jinan and Xuzhou are all located here.

小知识 Knowledge

华北平原主要是由黄河、淮河、海河三条大河带来的巨量泥沙逐渐填海而成的，是典型的冲积平原。

The North China Plain came into being because of the large amounts of mud and sand brought down by the Yellow, Huaihe and Haihe rivers filled in the sea. It is a typical alluvial plain.

1. 河北滦平县的田野
The field in Luanping County, Hebei Province
2. 华北平原
The North China Plain

长江中下游平原
The Middle and Lower Yangtze Valley Plain

长江中下游平原面积约20万平方千米，是中国的第三大平原。

The Middle and Lower Yangtze Valley Plain has an area of about 200,000 km^2 and is the third largest plain in China.

1. 长江中下游平原的水稻田
   Paddy fields on the Middle and Lower Yangtze Valley Plain
2. 油菜花
   Rape flower
3. 长江中下游平原是中国著名的鱼米之乡
   The Middle and Lower Yangtze Valley Plain is a famous land of fish and rice in China.

长江中下游平原地势低平，河湖密布，素有“水乡泽国”之称。这里水田连片，盛产水稻，淡水渔业发达，是中国著名的鱼米之乡。

The Middle and Lower Yangtze Valley Plain is low and flat, densely covered with rivers and lakes, and enjoying the reputation of a “water village”. This area has boundless paddy fields and developed freshwater fishery and is rich in paddy. It is a famous land of fish and rice in China.

小知识 Knowledge

长江中下游平原人口众多，城市密集，如武汉、长沙、南京、上海等重要城市都分布在这里，并且交通便利，经济繁荣。

The Middle and Lower Yangtze Valley Plain has a large population and densely distributed cities like Wuhan, Changsha, Nanjing and Shanghai. It also has very convenient transportation and a prosperous economy.

塔里木盆地
The Tarim Basin

1

塔里木盆地位于天山、昆仑山、阿尔金山与帕米尔高原之间，面积约53万平方千米，是中国也是世界上最大的内陆盆地。盆地四周被高山环绕，封闭得严严实实，气候极端干旱，干燥的风蚀和风积地貌发育十分典型。

The Tarim Basin, encircled by the Tianshan Mountains, Kunlun Mountains, Altyn Tagh Mountains and the Pamirs, and with a total area of about 530,000 km^2, is the largest inland basin in the world. Because of the mountain barriers, the weather there is extremely dry. It has a typical geomorphology of dry wind erosion and wind deposit.

小资料 Data

"塔里木"，过去认为是维吾尔语"田地"、"种田"的意思。新的研究成果认为，"塔里木"是"流入湖内和沙漠的支流"的意思。

"Tarim", in the past, was considered to mean "fields" or "cultivated lands" in the Uygur language. But more recent research shows that "Tarim" means "river branches flowing into lakes and deserts".

塔里木盆地从边缘到内部形成了典型的环状结构，由外向内依次为砾石戈壁带——绿洲带——沙漠。

盆地的外围是由碎石组成的戈壁滩。戈壁滩的透水性极强，夏季，高山冰雪的融水流到这里就渗到了地下，所以戈壁滩的地表总是干涸的。

在戈壁滩内侧，绿洲断断续续，组成一条环状的绿洲带。绿洲内水草丰茂，渠道纵横，林木成网，农田成片，经济发达，盆地内的人们主要居住在这里。

塔克拉玛干沙漠

塔克拉玛干沙漠位于塔里木盆地内部，东西长约1,000千米，南北宽约400千米，面积约33万平方千米，是中国面积最大的沙漠。

在塔克拉玛干沙漠上可以看到各种各样的沙丘，有的像新月，有的像波涛，高度一般超过100米，有的可达二三百米。

沙漠地区非常干旱，甚至终年无雨，生存条件极为恶劣。

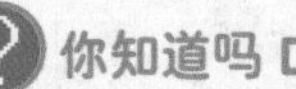

你知道吗 Do you know

塔里木盆地的地下埋藏着大量的石油，人们称它为"油海"。近年来，来这里考察的科学家和探险家越来越多。

Rich oil deposits are buried under the Tarim Basin so that people call it an "oil sea". In recent years, more and more scientists and explorers have traveled there for research.

A typical loop structure has formed from the edge to the interior of the Tarim Basin, moving in turn from the Gravel and Gobi Belt to the Oasis Belt and then desert.

The periphery of the Basin is Gobi land made up of stone fragments. The Gobi land is very permeable. In summer, the melted ice and snow from the high mountains flows down and permeates the ground so that the surface of the Gobi is always dry.

Within the Gobi land, there are intermittent oases forming a strip-like belt. Each oasis is rich in grass and water flowing through a network of channels and farmland, with many trees to provide shelter. This has helped the local economy to develop and the people of the basin mostly live here.

2

The Taklamakan Desert

The Taklamakan Desert, located in the Tarim Basin, is about 1,000 km long from east to west and about 400 km wide from south to north. It has an area of about 330,000 km² and is the largest desert in China.

Various dunes can be found in the Taklamakan Desert, some are like new moon, some like waves. The average height is more than 100 m and some can be 200 or 300 m high.

The desert area is very dry, with no rain at all throughout a year, making conditions for life extremely difficult.

1. 沙漠、戈壁和绿洲
Desert, Gobi and Oasis
2. 沙漠地区非常干旱，生存条件恶劣
The desert area is very dry, making conditions for life difficult.

准噶尔盆地
The Junggar Basin

1. 准噶尔东部油田
Eastern Junggar's oil field
2. 准噶尔盆地风光
The Junggar Basin

准噶尔盆地位于天山和阿尔泰山之间，面积约38万平方千米，是中国第二大盆地。它东高西低，是个半封闭型的盆地。

The Junggar Basin lies between the Tianshan Mountains and the Altai Mountains. It has an area of about 380,000 km^2 and is the second largest basin in China. It is a half-closed basin high in the east and low in the west.

盆地中心分布着中国的第二大沙漠——古尔班通古特沙漠。盆地的地下埋藏着丰富的石油，早在20世纪50年代就开发了著名的克拉玛依油田。

In the middle of the basin is located the second largest desert in China—the Badain Jaran Desert. There are rich oil deposits underground and early in the 1950s, the famous Karamay Oilfield was explored.

柴达木盆地
The Qaidam Basin

1. 青海盐湖
Salt Lake, Qinghai Province
2. 柴达木盆地底部平坦开阔
The bottom of the Qaidam Basin is very wide and flat.

柴达木盆地位于青藏高原东北部的青海省境内，面积约25万平方千米，是中国第三大盆地。盆地底部平均海拔2,600～3,000米，是中国海拔最高的大盆地。

The Qaidam Basin, the third largest basin in China, has an area of about 250,000 km^2, and is located in Qinghai Province northeast of the Qinghai-Tibet Plateau. The average altitude of the bottom of the basin is about 2,600 – 3,000 m, the highest in China.

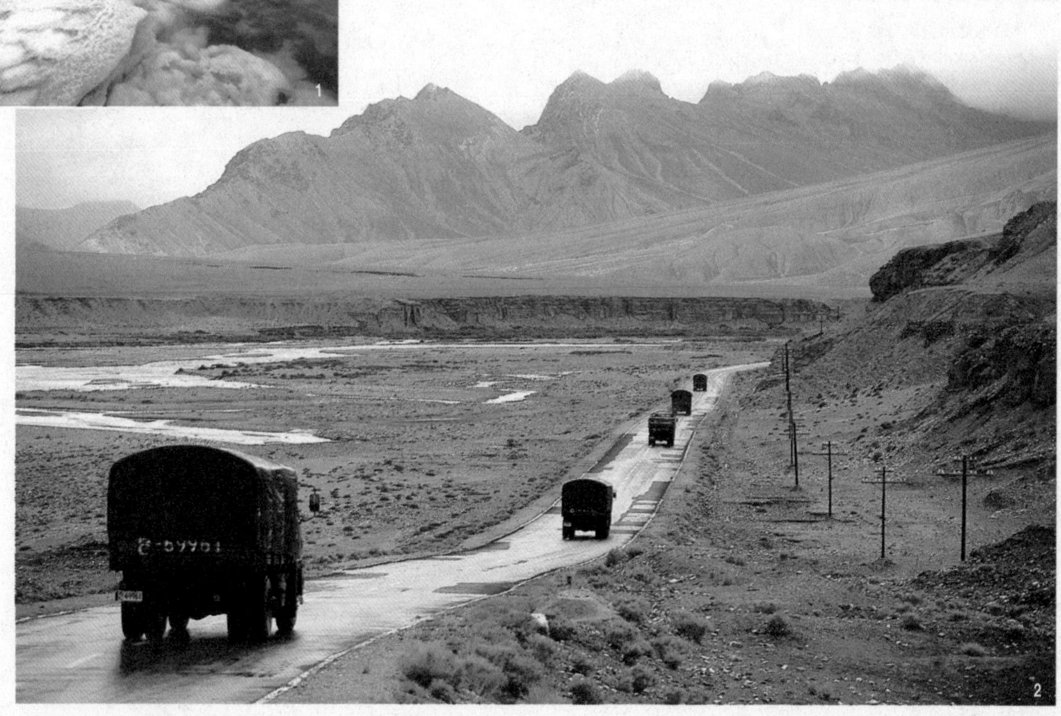

柴达木盆地盐碱地貌
The saline land of Qaidam Basin

盆地底部平坦开阔，骑马或驾车就像是在高原上行驶一样。

盆地内部有丰富的矿产资源，人们称它为“聚宝盆”。盐、石油、铅锌和硼砂是盆地中的“四大宝”。

这里的盐特别多，简直是盐的世界！大大小小的盐湖有100多个，食盐总储量有600亿吨之多！在这里我们可以看到用盐铺设的飞机场和用盐盖起的房屋。

The bottom of the basin is very wide and flat so that it feels like crossing an ordinary plateau.

There are rich mineral resources in the Qaidam Basin, such as the “four great treasures”: salt, oil, lead zinc and borax.

There is so much salt, in fact, that it is actually a salt world! There are more than 100 salt lakes. The total salt reserves reach 60 billion tn. Here we can see airport and houses built by salt.

你知道吗 Do you know

“柴达木”在蒙古语中是“盐泽”的意思。

“Qaidam” means “salt lake” in Mongolian language.

四川盆地
The Sichuan Basin

四川盆地是一个群山环绕的完整盆地，平均海拔500米左右，面积约为18万平方千米，是中国的第四大盆地。

The Sichuan Basin is an intact basin surrounded by mountains. With an average altitude of about 500 m and an area of about 180,000 km², it is the fourth largest basin in China.

1. 都江堰
The Dujiang Weirs
2. 山间的盆地
The basin surrounded by mountains

盆地的西北部有一片长约200千米，宽40～70千米的平原，这就是著名的成都平原。这里有举世闻名的都江堰工程，灌溉着肥沃的土地，自古农业发达，物产丰富，素有"天府之国"的美称。

盆地内气候冬暖夏热，温差小，雨量充沛，冬季多云雾。

There is a 200 km-long and 40 – 70 km-wide plain in the northwest of the basin, which is the famous Chengdu Plain where the world famous Dujiang Weirs have long irrigated the fertile land. Since ancient times, this area has enjoyed a reputation as a "land of plenty".

The climate of the basin is warm in winter and hot in summer, with small temperature difference and plenty of rain. In winter, it is mostly cloudy and foggy.

你知道吗 Do you know

盆地内部，丘陵起伏，从山上到山下，从石头到泥土，满山遍野都是紫红色的，所以人们称它为"紫色盆地"。

In the basin, the hills are undulating. From the top to the foot of the hills, from stones to earth, everywhere is purplish red, so that people call it the "purple basin".

长 江
Yangtze River

长江发源于青藏高原唐古拉山主峰——各拉丹冬雪峰，流经青海、西藏、四川、云南、重庆、湖北、湖南、江西、安徽、江苏、上海等11个省、市、自治区，注入东海，全长6,300多千米，为中国第一、世界第三长河。

The Yangtze River originates from the main peak of the Tanggula Mountains on the Qinghai-Tibet Plateau, and passes through 11 provinces, cities and autonomous regions of Qinghai, Tibet, Sichuan, Yunnan, Chongqing, Hubei, Hunan, Jiangxi, Anhui, Jiangsu and Shanghai, before finally flowing into the East China Sea. With a length of more than 6,300 km, it is the longest river in China and the third longest river in the world.

1. 长江是中国最长的河流
   Yangtze River is the longest river in China.
2. 青海长江源头各拉丹冬雪山脚下
   The foot of Geladaindong Snow Mountains lies the source of the Yangtze River in Qinghai Province.

长江上游落差大，水流急，有许多高山耸峙的峡谷地段，如虎跳峡、三峡等。

虎跳峡

虎跳峡位于云南省丽江纳西族自治县境内，长约16千米，两岸山岭高出江面3,000米以上，水流落差达200米，江水咆哮。江面最窄处不到30米，相传有巨虎一跃而过，所以称为“虎跳峡”。

长江出三峡后，进入中游的平原地区。这里江面变宽，水流减缓。多曲流、多支流、多湖泊是这一段的主要特征。

长江下游地区地势低平，江阔水深，是著名的鱼米之乡。长江入海口处，江面宽达80～90千米，水天一色，极为壮观。

长江不但具有巨大的航运价值，被称为“黄金水道”，而且两岸的自然风光绚丽多姿，名胜古迹众多。

长江流域物产丰富，经济发达。上海、南京、武汉、重庆等大城市都分布在这里。

1. 虎跳峡
   The Tiger-Jumping Gorge
2. 瞿塘峡
   The Qutang Gorge

The upper reaches of the Yangtze feature a big vertical drop, with torrents and many gorges flanked by towering mountains, such as the Tiger-Jumping Gorge, Three Gorges, and so on.

The Tiger-Jumping Gorge

Located in Lijiang Naxi Autonomous County of Yunnan Province, the Tiger-Jumping Gorge is about 16 km long. The mountains on both banks of the gorge rise over 3,000 m above the river and the drop of the roaring river reaches 200 m. At its narrowest point, the gorge is only 30 m wide. It is said that there was once a huge tiger that jumped over it, hence the name “Tiger-Jumping Gorge”.

2

After the Three Gorges, one reaches the plain area in the middle reaches of the river. Here the river broadens and the flow slows down. This part is characterized with many crooked streams, branches and lakes.

Known as the famous land of fish and rice, the lower reaches of the Yangtze River are low and flat, as well as broad and deep. At the spot where the Yangtze enters the sea, the river is 80 – 90 km wide, where the water and sky blend into one splendid color.

Reputed to be "Golden Watercourse", the Yangtze River has not only a high value for shipping, but also beautiful natural scenery and many scenic spots and historical sites.

The drainage area of the Yangtze River is rich in products and the economy is well developed. Many metropolises like Shanghai, Nanjing, Wuhan and Chongqing are distributed here.

黄　河
Yellow River

黄河发源于青海省巴颜喀拉山脉雅拉达泽山麓，流经青海、四川、甘肃、宁夏、内蒙古、山西、陕西、河南、山东等9个省、区，注入渤海，全长5,400多千米，是中国的第二长河。从地图上看，黄河呈一巨大的“几”字形。

The Yellow River originates from the foot of the Yagradagze Mountain of the Bayakala Range in Qinghai Province, passing through nine provinces and autonomous regions of Qinghai, Sichuan, Gansu, Ningxia, Inner Mongolia, Shanxi, Shaanxi, Henan and Shandong, and flowing into the Bohai Sea. Altogether it is over 5,400 km long and is the second longest river in China. Seen from the map, the Yellow River lies in a shape of "几".

1. 黄河壶口瀑布
   Hukou Waterfalls, Yellow River
2. 青海黄河源头人家
   The families who live at the source of the Yellow River, Qinghai Province

黄河上游有许多峡谷，如龙羊峡、刘家峡、青铜峡等。这些峡谷地带水力资源丰富，已建成龙羊峡等大型水电站。

黄河中游穿行于黄土高原，这里水土流失严重，河水中的泥沙含量大，形成了滚滚的“泥河”。

黄河下游主要流经低缓的华北平原，这里河道宽阔，水流变缓，泥沙在此大量沉积，形成了河床比两岸高的“地上河”。

壶口瀑布

壶口瀑布位于山西和陕西的交界处，黄河将此处的河底冲刷出一道30～50米宽的深槽。北来的河水进入槽内，激流汹涌，夺路下泻，形成15～20米高的瀑布，响声如雷，景色十分壮观，它就像沸腾的开水从巨壶倾倒而出，所以称为“壶口”瀑布。

There are many gorges on its upper reaches, such as the Dragon and Sheep Gorge, the Family Liu Gorge and the Bronze Gorge. Such areas have an abundance of water resources and large-scale hydroelectric power stations have been built.

The middle reaches of the Yellow River flow through the Loess Plateau, where there is a serious problem of soil erosion. This part of the river contains large amount of sand, forming a powerful "mud river".

The drainage area of the lower reaches of the Yellow River covers the North China Plain, where the river broadens, the flow slows down and the mud and sand deposits form a "hanging river", where the riverbed is actually higher than the surrounding land beyond the built-up banks.

The Hukou (Kettle's Mouth) Falls

The Hukou Falls are located at the juncture of Shanxi and Shaanxi provinces, where there is a 30 – 50 m-wide deep gully scoured by the Yellow River. The turbulent river from north rushes down into the gully, forming a 15 – 20 m-high fall rumbling like thunder. The fall rushes down like boiling water pouring down from a huge kettle, hence its name.

你知道吗 Do you know

黄河是中华民族的母亲河，黄河流域被称为中华民族的摇篮，也是世界文明的发祥地之一。相传中华民族的始祖之一——黄帝就出生在这里。

The Yellow River is the Mother River of the Chinese people. The drainage area of the Yellow River is honored as the cradle of Chinese nation and also one of the original places of world civilization. It is said that Huangdi (Yellow Emperor, legendary ruler and ancestor of the Chinese nation) was born here.

1. 九曲黄河
   The Yellow River in zigzag course
2. 龙羊峡水电站
   Dragon and Sheep Gorge Hydropower Station

雅鲁藏布江
Yarlung Zangbo River

雅鲁藏布江是中国最高的大河之一，发源于喜马拉雅山北麓，在中国境内长2,057千米。

The Yarlung Zangbo River is one of the highest rivers in China, originating from the northern peaks of the Himalayas. The part flowing through Chinese territory is altogether 2,057 km long.

1

雅鲁藏布江的上游是高寒地带。这里河谷开阔，大部分是平浅谷地，水流缓慢，多湖塘沼泽。原始的大面积草场是天然的动物乐园，生活着藏羚羊、岩羊、野驴、野牦牛等许多野生动物。

中游地带，河谷宽窄相间，一放一束，呈串珠状分布。

下游地区，江水绕过喜马拉雅山东段的高山，折向南流，形成了世界上最大的峡谷——雅鲁藏布大峡谷。它呈马蹄形，以雄伟、险峻和奇特闻名于世。

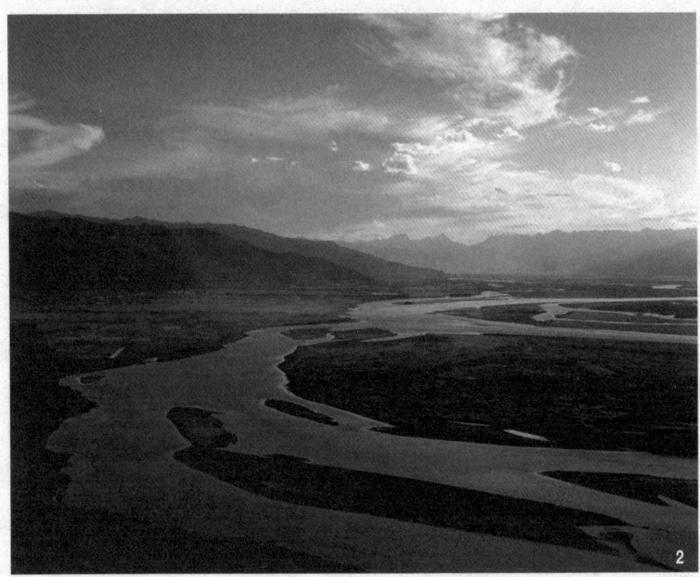
2

1. 雅鲁藏布大峡谷
The Yarlung Zangbo Canyon
2. 雅鲁藏布江上游水流缓慢，多湖、塘、沼泽
The upper reaches of the Yarlung Zangbo River have many broad, flat and shallow river valleys.

The upper reaches of the Yarlung Zangbo River lie in a frigid zone. Here are broad river valleys, most of which are flat and shallow. The current here is slow and there are many lakes and swamps. The large area of aboriginal grassland is a paradise for wild animals, such as the Tibetan antelope, blue sheep, wild donkeys and wild yaks.

The middle reaches of the river alternate between narrow and broad river valleys that are distributed like a string of beads.

In the lower reaches, the river rounds a high mountain in the eastern part of the Himalayas and turns south, forming the largest canyon in the world—the Yarlung Zangbo Canyon. It is in the shape of a horse's hoof and has become world famous for its majesty, steepness and peculiar charm.

小资料 Data

雅鲁藏布江流域是藏族文化的发源地，有拉萨、日喀则、江孜和林芝等重要文化和旅游城市。

The drainage area of the Yarlung Zangbo River is the birthplace of Tibetan culture. There are many cities of cultural and tourist significance, such as Lhasa, Xigaze, Jiangzi and Linzhi.

京杭运河
Beijing-Hangzhou Canal

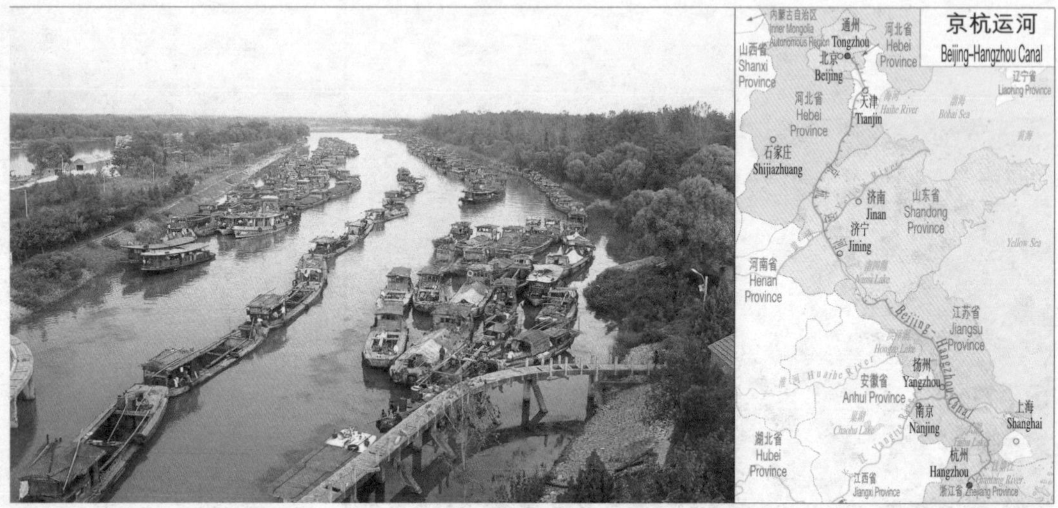

京杭大运河从江苏徐州城边穿过

The Grand Beijing-Hangzhou Canal passes by Xuzhou City, Jiangsu Province.

小资料 Data

古代开凿京杭运河主要是为了将南方的粮食等物资运到北方。1911年津浦铁路开通后，此运河的交通价值大大下降。现在，除江苏、浙江境内的河段仍是重要的水上运输线外，其他地段已不能通航。

In ancient times, the Beijing-Hangzhou Canal was dug to ship grain and other materials from the south to the north. In 1911, after the Tianjin-Huangpu Railway was put into use, the transportation value of the canal decreased drastically. Now, except for the part in Jiangsu and Zhejiang where it is still an important transportation route, the rest of the canal is no longer open to shipping.

京杭运河北起北京，南到杭州，纵贯北京、天津、河北、山东、江苏、浙江等6个省、市，沟通了海河、黄河、淮河、长江、钱塘江五大水系，全长1,782千米，是世界上开凿最早、路线最长的人工运河。

The Beijing-Hangzhou Canal extends from Beijing in the north to Hangzhou in the south, covering six provinces and cities of Beijing, Tianjin, Hebei, Shandong, Jiangsu and Zhejiang, and connecting the five great water systems of the Haihe, Yellow, Huaihe, Yangtze and Qiantang rivers. With a total length of 1,782 km, it is the earliest and longest man-made canal in the world.

鄱阳湖
Poyang Lake

鄱阳湖位于江西省北部，北通长江，面积3,583平方千米，是中国最大的淡水湖。

Poyang Lake, the largest freshwater lake in China, is located in northern Jiangxi Province, and connected to the Yangtze River in the north. It has an area of 3,583 km^2.

鄱阳湖渔民归航
Fisherman returns to the Poyang Lake.

小资料 Data

鄱阳湖古称彭泽、彭湖，后因湖中有鄱阳山而改为鄱阳湖。

Poyang Lake was called the Peng Damp or Peng Lake in ancient times; later, because there is the Poyang Mountain in the middle of the lake, it was renamed.

壮阔的鄱阳湖与湖口的石钟山、湖滨的庐山及滔滔奔流的长江一起构成了一幅以大湖、名山、巨川为中心内容的宏伟画卷。

鄱阳湖水面广阔，饵料丰富，气候湿润，是白鹤、天鹅、白鹳等多种珍稀鸟类的理想越冬场所。如今，湖畔兴建了候鸟观赏台，"湖畔观鸟"已成为湖区的一大胜景。

The broad Poyang Lake, together with Stone Bell Mountain at the entrance of the lake, Mt. Lu on its banks and the surging Yangtze River, forms a splendid picture.

The lake is very broad and rich in fish resources. It is also an ideal place for white cranes, swans and many other rare birds to spend their winters due to its humid weather. A terrace has now been built on the side of the lake for viewing the migratory birds, and it has become one of the great scenic spots in the area.

1. 鄱阳湖是鸟类的理想越冬场所
Poyang Lake is an ideal place for many birds to spend their winters.
2. "江南三大名楼"之一的滕王阁位于鄱阳湖畔
One of the three famous pavilions in the south reaches of the Yangtze River, Teng Wangge Pavilion, sits right beside the Poyang Lake.

洞庭湖
Dongting Lake

1. 岳阳楼
   Yueyang Tower
2. 洞庭湖风光
   Scenery of Dongting Lake

洞庭湖位于湖南省北部、长江南岸，面积2,820平方千米，是中国的第二大淡水湖。

China's second largest freshwater lake, Dongting Lake, has an area of 2,820 km^2 and is located in the northern Hunan Province to the south of the Yangtze River.

洞庭湖区山川秀美，人杰地灵，名胜古迹较多。著名的岳阳楼就坐落于此，素有“洞庭天下水，岳阳天下楼”之誉。

There are graceful mountains and rivers, outstanding personages and many famous scenic spots and historical sites in the Dongting Lake area. The famous Yueyang Tower, immortalized in the lines, “the most beautiful lake under heaven is Dongting, the greatest tower under heaven is Yueyang”, is located here.

据唐、宋时期的文献记载，洞庭湖方圆七八百里，故有后来的“八百里洞庭”之说。洞庭湖原是中国第一大淡水湖，但由于泥沙长期淤积等原因，湖面日趋减小，现在的面积已不足当时的1/2。

It is recorded in ancient documents that, during the Tang and Song dynasties (618 – 1279 AD), Dongting Lake was about 700-800 *li* (about 400 km) in width and length. Therefore, it was called “800-*li* Dongting”. The Dongting Lake used to be the largest freshwater lake in China, but because the mud and sand deposited over time, it has shrunk to about half its original size.

太　湖
Taihu Lake

太湖位于江苏、浙江两省交界处，面积2,425平方千米，是中国的第三大淡水湖。

湖区有48岛，72峰，湖光山色，相映生辉，有“太湖天下秀”之称。

Taihu Lake, the third largest freshwater lake in China, has an area of 2,425 km^2 and lies at the juncture of Jiangsu and Zhejiang provinces.

There are 48 islets and 72 peaks in the lake area. The lake and the mountains set each other off delightfully. It has a reputation of "the most graceful lake under heaven".

你知道吗 Do you know

鄱阳湖、洞庭湖、太湖、洪泽湖、巢湖被称为中国五大淡水湖。

Poyang Lake, Dongting Lake, Taihu Lake, Hongze Lake and Chaohu Lake are called the five great lakes in China.

1. 太湖渔歌
   Taihu Lake and the old fishing boats
2. 风光优美的太湖
   The splendid Taihu Lake
3. 春到太湖
   Springtime at Taihu Lake
4. 鼋头渚是观赏太湖风光的绝佳处
   Yuan Touzhu is an ideal place to view the Taihu Lake.

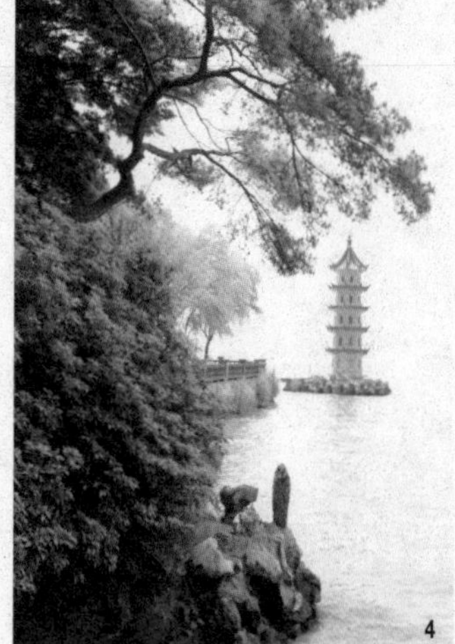

太湖平原气候温和湿润，土壤肥沃，水网密布，是“鱼米之乡”。

太湖周围有苏州、无锡等著名的城市。

The Taihu Lake Plain has a mild and moist climate, fertile soil and a network of waterways that create “a land of fish and rice”.

Nearby are such famous cities as Suzhou and Wuxi.

青海湖
Qinghai Lake

青海湖，古代称为“西海”，位于青海省东北部，面积4,583平方千米，是中国最大的咸水湖，也是中国第一大湖。

Qinghai Lake, called "West Sea" in ancient times, is located in the northeast of Qinghai Province. With an area of 4,583 km^2, it is the biggest salt lake and also the largest lake in China.

1

小知识 Knowledge

青海湖，蒙语叫"库库诺尔"，藏语叫"错温波"，都是"青色的海"的意思。青海湖水色青绿，湖滨水草丰美，不少地方已开辟为牧场和农场。

Qinghai Lake is called "Koko Nor" in Mongolian language and "Tsuwabo" in Tibetan, which both mean "blue green sea". The lake is blue green and has an abundance of aquatic life living along its banks. Many places have been developed into livestock farms and pastures.

冬季，湖面封冻，像一面镜子，在阳光下闪闪发光。三月底湖面开始解冻，几场大风过后，湖冰被吹到岸边堆积，犹如冰山，是湖区一大奇景。夏秋季节，湖区山青草绿，各种各样的花草将湖滨点缀得非常漂亮。

湖中的鸟岛和海心山是候鸟最为集中的地方，多时可达10万只。

鸟岛

初夏是到鸟岛观光的最好季节，这时的鸟岛，遍地是各种各样的鸟巢和五光十色的鸟蛋。天上飞的是鸟，地下跑的是鸟，水中游的还是鸟，热闹非凡，非常壮观。

In winter, the lake is frozen, and it shines like a mirror in the sun. Harsh winds can pile up the ice on the banks in fantastic shapes. At the end of March, the ice begins to melt. In summer and autumn, the mountains and grass turn green, and beautiful flowers and grasses appear.

Bird Islet in the middle of the lake and the Haixin (Heart of the Sea) Mountain attract migratory birds whose number sometimes reaches 100,000.

Bird Islet

Early summer is the best time to visit Bird Islet. At this time, it is covered with various birds' nests and colorful birds' eggs. Birds are flying, running and swimming everywhere, creating a busy and spectacular scene.

1. 青海湖冬景
   Qinghai Lake in winter
2. 青海湖中的鸟岛和海心山是候鸟最为集中的地方
   The Bird Islet and Haixin Mountain of Qinghai Lake have the highest concentration of migratory birds.

台湾岛
Taiwan Island

台湾岛位于中国东南海面上，面积约3.5万平方千米，是中国第一大岛。

Taiwan Island, located in the Southeast China Sea, with an area of about 35,000 km^2, is the largest island in China.

1

2

小资料 Data

台湾自古以来就是中国不可分割的一部分，三国时期称它为夷洲，明朝才叫台湾。历史上多次受外来侵略，1662年郑成功收复了台湾。

Taiwan has been an inseparable part of China's territory since ancient times. In the Three Kingdoms Period (220 – 280 AD) it was called *Yizhou*. Not until the Ming Dynasty (1368 – 1644 AD) was it named Taiwan. It has been invaded many times. In 1662, Zheng Chenggong (1624 – 1662 AD) reoccupied Taiwan.

台湾有"八景十二胜"。八景是玉山积雪、阿里云海、双潭秋月、大屯春色、安平夕照、清水断崖、鲁阁幽峡和澎湖渔火。

Taiwan has eight scenic spots and 12 attractions. The eight scenic spots are Accumulated Snow on the Jade Mountain, Sea of Cloud in Ali, Autumn Moon of Double Ponds, Spring Scenery in Datun, Sunset in Anping, Precipice in Qingshui, Remote Canyon of Luge and Lights on Fishing Boats in Penghu.

台湾经济发达，交通便利，美丽富饶，名胜古迹众多，如阿里山、日月潭、乌来瀑布等都是著名的旅游胜地。

阿里山

阿里山主要有森林、云海、日出和樱花四大奇观。

故宫博物院

台北市的故宫博物院是亚洲古代文物中心之一，院内藏有许多中国古代艺术珍品。

3

1. 台北
Taipei
2. 玉山
Jade Mountain
3. 台北的故宫博物院
The Palace Museum in Taipei

日月潭

日月潭位于台湾中部玉山以北，是台湾第一天然大湖。

湖畔有许多亭台楼阁。潭西的涵碧楼是观赏湖光山色的好地方，潭南的玄奘寺是台湾的佛教胜地。

野柳

台湾岛东北海岸野柳的岩石形状非常奇特，有“女王头”、“仙女鞋”、“乳房石”等48景，令游客惊叹不已，被称为“出自上帝之手的杰作”。五颜六色的贝壳和海胆以及美人蕉、龙舌兰等海岸植物，使这里成为一个天然的海岸公园。

Taiwan has a developed economy, convenient transportation, many famous scenic spots and historical sites, such as the Ali Mountain, the Sun and Moon Lake, Wulai Falls, and so on. It is very beautiful and rich in resources.

Ali Mountain

Ali Mountain has four wonders: forest, sea of cloud, sunrise and cherry blossom.

1. 台北孔庙
   The Taipei Confucius Temple
2. 野柳“女王头”
   Yeliu “Queen's head”
3. 日月潭
   The Sun and Moon Lake
4. 高雄
   Kaohsiung
5. 上班时间的台北街头
   Rush hour in Taipei

Palace Museum

The Palace Museum in Taipei is one of the centers of ancient Asian cultural relics, in which are housed many precious ancient Chinese art works.

The Sun and Moon Lake

The Sun and Moon Lake, the largest natural lake in Taiwan, is located to the north of the Jade Mountain in the middle of Taiwan.

On its banks are many pavilions, terraces and towers. The Hanbi Tower to the west of the lake is a good place to view the lake and mountains. To the south, the Xuanzang Temple is the holiest place of Buddhism in Taiwan.

Yeliu

At Yeliu, on the northeast shore of Taiwan Island, there are many stones in very special shapes, such as "queen's head", "fairy lady's shoes", "breast stones" and so on, 48 attractions in all, which amaze tourists and are called "masterpieces made by God". Shells and sea urchins in various colors, cannas, maguey and other seashore plants have created a natural seashore park.

小知识 Knowledge

日月潭中有个美丽的小岛，叫光华岛，它把日月潭分为南北两半，北半湖形状像太阳，南半湖像一弯新月，所以叫"日月潭"。

There is a beautiful islet in the Sun and Moon Lake, which is named Splendor Islet. It divides the Sun and Moon Lake into southern and northern parts. The northern part looks like the sun, and the southern one is similar to a crescent; therefore, it is called "the Sun and Moon Lake".

海南岛
Hainan Island

海南岛在中国的南部，面积32,200多平方千米。北隔琼州海峡同雷州半岛相望，是中国第二大岛。

Hainan Island, the second largest island in China, lies in the far south, with an area of over 32,200 km^2. It faces the Leizhou Peninsula across the Qiongzhou Strait to the north.

小资料 Data

海南岛原来是和大陆连在一起的，后因琼州海峡沉陷，才与大陆分离。琼州海峡最窄处只有18千米。

Hainan Island was originally connected to the land, until the land sank to let in the sea and form Qiongzhou Strait, whose narrowest point is only 18 km wide.

1. 三亚鹿回头的传说雕像
   The statue of Deer Looking Back, Sanya City
2. 海南椰风海韵
   Natural scenery of Hainan Island
3. 水清沙幼的三亚海滩
   Lovely beach of Sanya
4. "天涯海角"
   "End of the Earth"

1

2

3

4

海南岛的地形中间高，四周低。五指山是岛上最著名的山脉，从东南方望去，其主峰形似五指，因此而得名。

海南岛到处是一派热带风光。这里有大片的热带森林，植物种类繁多，终年常绿。另外还有许多独特的生物现象，如板状根、老茎生花等。

海南岛是橡胶、椰子、油棕、剑麻、胡椒等热带经济作物的主要产地。

海南岛是著名的旅游胜地，被称为南海上的一颗"明珠"。特别是南部的三亚市，碧水蓝天，景色迷人。牙龙湾、大东海、天涯海角、鹿回头等著名景点，每天都吸引着众多的国内外游人。

Hainan is high in the middle and low on all sides. Five-Fingers Mountain is the most famous mountain on the island. Seen from the southeast, the main peak is like five fingers.

One will enjoy tropical scenery everywhere on Hainan. There is a large area of tropical forest, a variety of evergreen plants, plus many special biological phenomena, such as plate-like roots, blossoms on old stems and so on.

Hainan is the main production area for tropical cash crops such as rubber, coconuts, oil palms, sisal and pepper, etc.

It is a famous tourist place, reputed to be a "pearl" in the South China Sea. Moreover, Sanya City in the south has green seawater, blue sky and charming scenery. Many famous scenic spots such as Tooth Dragon Bay, Great East Sea, End of the Earth and Deer Looking Back, attract thousands of visitors every day.

你知道吗 Do you know

海南岛的资源很丰富，这里有中国最著名的富铁矿和著名的莺歌海盐场。从珠江口到北部湾一带的海盆中，还蕴藏着丰富的天然气资源。

Hainan Island has an abundance of resources. These include the most famous iron ore in China, the renowned Yinggehai Salt Field, and the rich natural gas fields that lie under the sea basin from the mouth of the Pearl River to Beibu Bay.

南海诸岛
The South China Sea Islands

在中国的南海海面上，散布着众多的岛礁暗沙，总称为南海诸岛。

南海诸岛由东沙群岛、西沙群岛、中沙群岛、南沙群岛及黄岩岛组成。

The South China Sea is scattered with many islands, reefs and submerged shoals to which the general name South China Sea Islands is given.

The South China Sea Islands are made up of the East Sand Islands, West Sand Islands, Middle Sand Islands, South Sand Islands and Yellow Rock Island.

南海西沙
West Sand Islands of the South China Sea

南海诸岛处于太平洋和印度洋、亚洲和大洋洲海上航运的要冲位置，在交通和国防上都有重要的意义。很早以前，中华民族的祖先就在南海诸岛上开始活动并修筑了相应的建筑，中国对南海诸岛拥有主权。

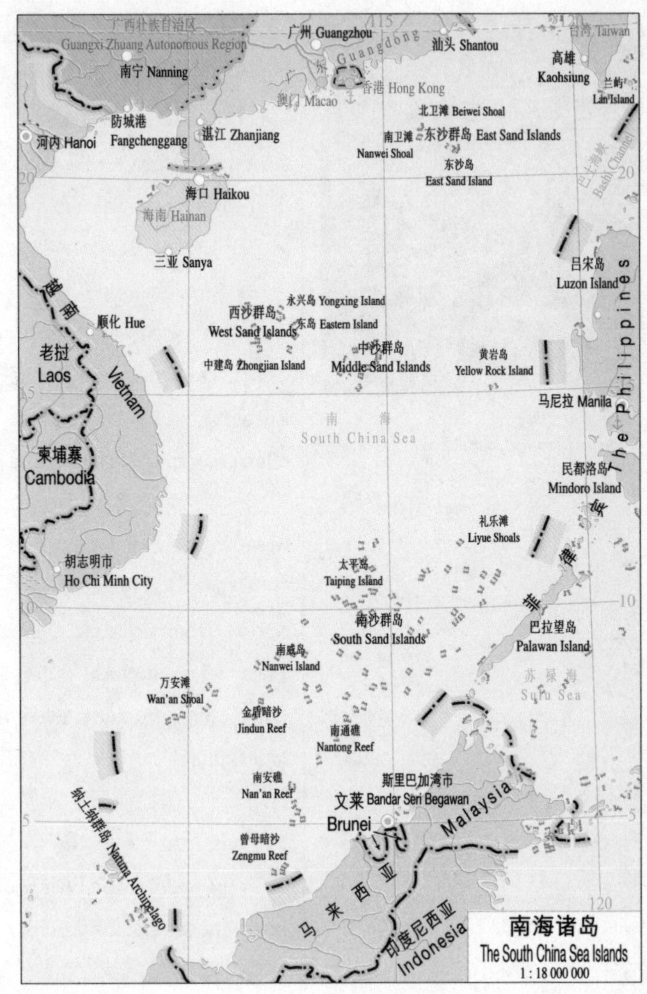

东沙群岛

东沙群岛由东沙岛及南卫滩、北卫滩组成。附近海域水产丰富，有海参、海胆、海星、蚌蛤和海人参草等。中国很早就在岛上建立了观象台和灯塔。

西沙群岛

西沙群岛是南海诸岛中岛屿最多的群岛。岛上生长着多种热带植物，如棕榈、椰子、木瓜、香蕉等。附近海域出产海龟、海参、金枪鱼等水产品，每到鱼汛期，广东、海南一带的渔船便云集于此进行捕捞。

中沙群岛

中沙群岛是一群尚未露出海面的珊瑚礁滩，距海平面约有一二十米。由于珊瑚礁映衬的结果，这一带的海水呈现着微绿的颜色。

南沙群岛

南沙群岛由分布很广、数量很多的岛、礁、暗沙组成，主要有太平岛等。岛上生长着椰子、木瓜等多种热带植物，附近海域也是南海重要的渔场之一。南端的曾母暗沙位于北纬4度附近，是中国领土最南的地方。

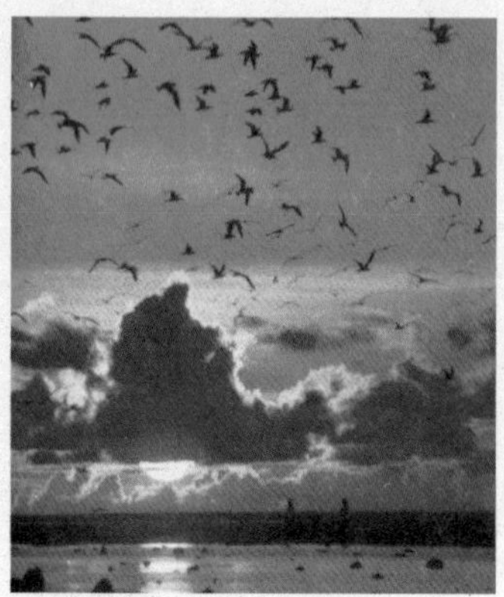

西沙夕照
Sunset at the West Sand Islands

The South China Sea Islands stand at the crossroads of the shipping lanes between Pacific and Indian oceans, Asia and Oceania, and are of great importance to transportation and national defense. Long ago, the ancestors of the Chinese people began to live there so that China has always had sovereignty over the area.

East Sand Islands

East Sand Islands comprise East Sand Island, Nanwei Shoal and Beiwei Shoal. The surrounding waters are rich in aquatic products, such as sea cucumber, sea urchin, starfish, mussels, clams and sea ginseng weeds, etc. China has an observatory and beacon on the islands.

West Sand Islands

West Sand Islands form the largest such group in the South China Sea. Various tropical plants, such as palm, coconut, pawpaw and banana grow there, while the local waters produce turtles, sea cucumbers, tunny and other aquatic products. Every fishing season, boats arrive from Guangdong and Hainan.

Middle Sand Islands

The Middle Sand Islands are a group of coral reef shoals lying 10 to 20 m below the sea surface. Against the background of the coral reefs, the seawater looks slightly green.

South Sand Islands

The South Sand Islands form a widely distributed, large group of islands, reefs and submerged shoals. The major island is called Taiping Island. On the islands grow coconuts, pawpaw and many other tropical plants, while the surrounding seas are an important fishing ground. The Zengmu Reef are located close to the 4th parallel of northern latitude, the most southern point of Chinese territory.

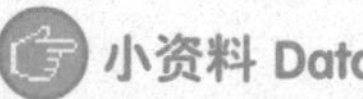

小资料 Data

南海诸岛附近海域，蕴藏着丰富的石油资源。较大的岛上都有很厚的鸟粪层，是鲣鸟的粪便堆积而成的，含磷量很高，是很好的肥料。

The maritime areas near the South China Sea Islands contain abundant oil reserves. The larger islands are covered in thick layer of bird dung, mainly from the brown booby, which has high phosphor content and is a very good fertilizer.

交通与水利

Transportation and Water Conservancy

铁　路
Railways

铁路是中国最重要的运输方式，到2000年底，铁路营业里程达6.86万千米，居世界第三位。

Railways provide a vital transportation mode in China. By the end of 2000, there were 68,600 km of track in use, the third longest in the world.

中国铁路干线可以分为南北干线和东西干线两大组，在南北干线和东西干线的交叉或衔接处，形成了许多重要的铁路枢纽，如北京、上海、天津、重庆、哈尔滨、徐州、西安、武汉等。东西干线主要有京包—包兰线、陇海—兰新线、沪杭—浙赣—湘黔—贵昆线；

南北干线主要有京哈—京广线、京沪线、京九线、焦柳线、宝成—成昆线等。这“三横”、“五纵”构成了中国铁路干线的主要骨架。

京广铁路北起北京，南到广州，穿过河北、河南、湖北、湖南、广东五省，全长2,324千米，是纵贯中国南北的交通大动脉，全线货运、客运都十分繁忙。

京沪铁路是纵贯中国东部地区的主要铁路干线，贯穿北京、天津、上海三个直辖市以及河北、山东、安徽、江苏四省，是首都北京通向华东地区的主要干线，全长1,462千米。京沪沿线经济繁荣，城镇密布。

京九铁路，从北京到香港的九龙，是介于京广、京沪两条纵向干线之间的又一条南北大动脉，对增强首都北京与香港以及南北方向的联系具有重要意义。

陇海—兰新铁路，东起连云港，西至西北重镇兰州，长1,736千米，这段称陇海线；由兰州向西至乌鲁木齐，长1,904千米，这段称兰新线。兰新线现已向西延伸至阿拉山口，与哈萨克斯坦铁路相连，成为了亚欧大陆桥的一个组成部分。陇海—兰新铁路是横贯中国东西的交通大动脉，对沟通东部与西部、沿海与内地、中国与欧洲的联系以及西部大开发等，都具有极其重要的意义。

青藏铁路，从青海西宁经格尔木到西藏拉萨（西宁—格尔木段已建成通车，格尔木—拉萨段正在建设之中），全长1,118千米。它的建成将结束西藏无铁路的历史。

小资料 Data

从1997年4月1日开始，中国在主要铁路干线上实行了三次大提速，现在，1,500千米路程以内的两地，可以做到“朝发夕至”。

From April 1, 1997 onwards, China has speeded up the running of trains on the main trunk railways three times. Now, one can "depart at night and arrive at the destination in the early morning" if the distance between two places is within 1,500 km.

China's trunk railways can be divided into two groups running south-north and east-west. There are many important hubs where lines meet such as, Beijing, Shanghai, Tianjin, Chongqing, Harbin, Xuzhou, Xi'an and Wuhan. The east-west trunk railways include such lines as Beijing-Baotou, Baotou-Lanzhou, Lianyungang-Lanzhou, Lanzhou-Urumqi, Shanghai-Hangzhou, Hangzhou-Nanchang, Zhuzhou-Guiyang and Guizhou-Kunming. The

北京西客站
Beijing West Railway Station

1. 中国铁路四通八达，对促进东南西北经济繁荣起着很大作用
China's extensive railway system helps to boost economy.
2. 上海磁悬浮列车，是中国新一代高速列车
Shanghai Magnetic Levitation Train marks the new generation of high-speed transport in China.

south-north trunk railways mainly include the Beijing-Harbin, Beijing-Guangzhou, Beijing-Shanghai, Beijing-Kowloon, Jiaozuo-Liuzhou, Baoji-Chengdu and Chengdu-Kunming lines. These lines form the basic framework of Chinese trunk railways.

The Beijing-Guangzhou line extends from the nation's capital in the north to Guangzhou in the south, passing through Hebei, Henan, Hubei, Hunan and Guangdong provinces. It covers 2,324 km and is the main artery of communications from north to south, carrying heavy loads of goods and passengers.

The Beijing-Shanghai line is the major trunk route in eastern China, linking the cities of Beijing, Tianjin and Shanghai and the four provinces of Hebei, Shandong, Anhui and Jiangsu, it has a total length of 1,462 km. There are many cities along this line and this part is the most prosperous region in China.

The Beijing-Kowloon line is another major north-south railway. It bears great importance in strengthening the connection between the nation's capital and Hong Kong.

The Longhai-Lanxin Railway has two parts. One part, called the Longhai Line, extends from Lianyungang in the east to Lanzhou in the northwest and has a length of 1,736 km; the other part, called the Lanxin Line, is about 1,904 km long, and extends from Lanzhou westward to Urumqi in Xinjiang. Now, the Lanxin Line has further extended westward to the Ala Mountain Pass. Connecting to the Kazakhstan rail system, it has become a key component in the Asia-Europe continental bridge. The Longhai-Lanxin Railway, traversing China from east to west, has an important role to play in western development and in developing a land transport route to Europe.

The 1,118-km-long Qinghai-Tibet Railway, from Xining in Qinghai Province and passing through Golmud to Lhasa in Tibet (the part from Xining to Golmud is already operational, while the remainder is under construction), will finally give Tibet its first rail link with the rest of the country.

公 路
Roads

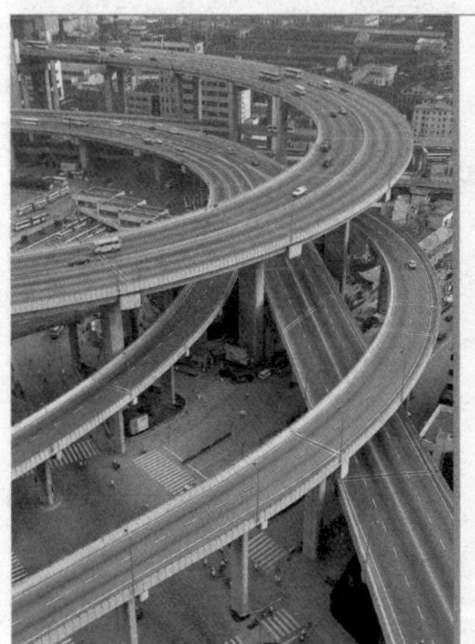
上海高速公路
Shanghai Expressway

中华人民共和国成立以后，公路建设发展迅速，公路运输网已遍布全国各地，实现了"县县通公路"。到2000年底，公路通车里程已达140多万千米。

Since the founding of the People's Republic of China in 1949, road construction has developed rapidly so that the transportation network has spread all over the country and every county has been connected by road. By the end of 2000, 1.4 million km of roads were open to traffic.

中国主要高速公路和西部主要公路
China's Major Expressways and Major Road in the West of China

	霍尔果斯 Korgas	29	武汉 Wuhan
	乌鲁木齐 Urumqi	30	合肥 Hefei
	红其拉甫达坂 Kunjirap Daban	31	南京 Nanjing
	普兰 Burang	32	上海 Shanghai
	聂拉木 Nyalam	33	杭州 Hangzhou
	拉萨 Lhasa	34	宁波 Ningbo
	格尔木 Golmod	35	长沙 Changsha
	西宁 Xining	36	南昌 Nanchang
	兰州 Lanzhou	37	福州 Fuzhou
	银川 Yinchuan	38	台北 Taipei
	成都 Chengdu	39	高雄 Kaohsiung
	重庆 Chongqing	40	厦门 Xiamen
	贵阳 Guiyang	41	广州 Guangzhou
	瑞丽 Ruili	42	南宁 Nanning
	昆明 Kunming	43	湛江 Zhanjiang
	河口 Hekou	44	海口 Haikou
	友谊关 Youyiguan	45	澳门 Macao
	满洲里 Manzhouli	46	香港 Hong Kong
	二连浩特 Erenhot	47	同江 Tongjiang
	呼和浩特 Hohhot	48	哈尔滨 Harbin
	北京 Beijing	49	绥芬河 Suifen River
	天津 Tianjin	50	长春 Changchun
	太原 Taiyuan	51	珲春 Hunchun
	石家庄 Shijiazhuang	52	沈阳 Shenyang
	济南 Jinan	53	丹东 Dandong
	西安 Xi'an	54	大连 Dalian
	郑州 Zhengzhou	55	青岛 Qingdao
	宜昌 Yichang	56	连云港 Lianyungang

1. 上海杨浦大桥
Yangpu Bridge, Shanghai
2. 北京四元桥
Siyuan Bridge, Beijing

从20世纪80年代后期开始建设高速公路，到2000年底，中国大陆的高速公路总长度达1.6万千米。北京、上海、天津、沈阳、大连、武汉、南京、广州、深圳等主要城市都开通了高速公路。

From late 1980s, when expressways began to be constructed, to the end of 2000, a total of 16,000 km of expressways had been completed. Many of the major cities like Beijing, Shanghai, Tianjin, Shenyang, Dalian, Wuhan, Nanjing, Guangzhou and Shenzhen all have their expressway networks.

航　空
Aviation

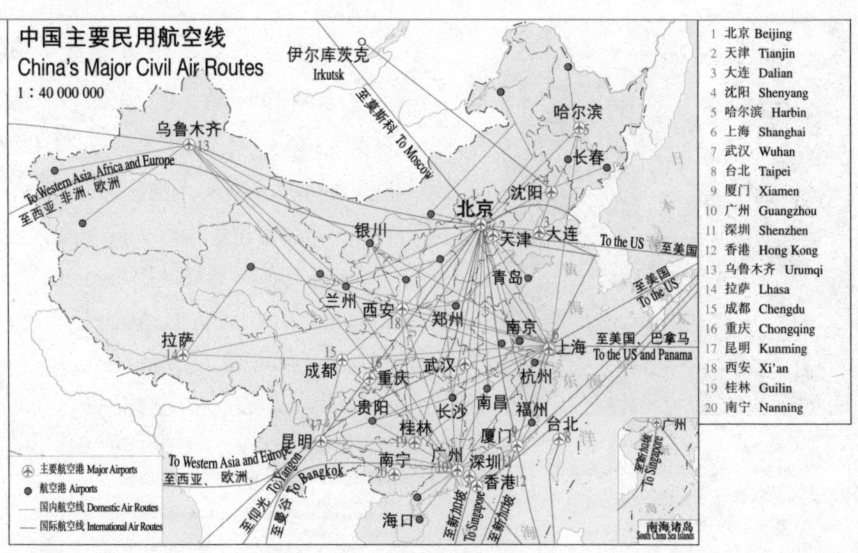

1. 北京首都机场
   Beijing Capital International Airport
2. 目前中国各主要城市之间航空线路均已开通
   Currently, main cities of China are all open to air traffic.

航空已成为中国重要的交通运输方式，到2000年底，国内民用航线已达1,000多条，主要城市之间都可通航，人们乘飞机出行已司空见惯。国际航线有120多条，通往世界各地的许多城市，北京、上海、广州、香港等是重要的国际航空港。

Air transport is now an important mode of travel. By the end of 2000, the number of civil air routes in China had exceeded 1,000. Main cities are all open to air traffic. It's very common that people go on trips by plane. There are over 120 international air routes opened up to other parts of the world. Beijing, Shanghai, Guangzhou and Hong Kong are among the most important international airports.

水　运
Water Transport

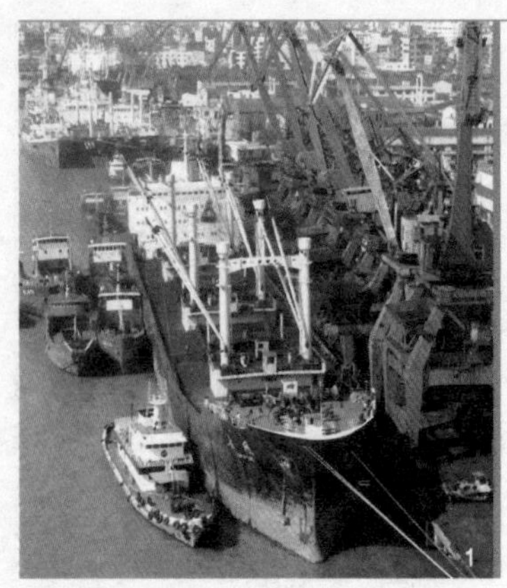

中国水运的发展历史十分悠久，远在商代就有了帆船。隋朝大运河的开通，为南北水上运输提供了极大的便利。明朝郑和七次下西洋，远及非洲东部沿海。

China's water transport has a long history. Early in the Shang Dynasty (1600 – 1046 BC) there were sailing boats. The great canal in the Sui Dynasty (581 – 618 AD) provided great convenience for south-north water transport. In the Ming Dynasty (1368 – 1644 AD), Zheng He (1371 – 1433 AD) navigated across seas seven times and reached the eastern coast of Africa in one of his voyages.

1. 上海浦东煤炭运输码头
   Shanghai Pudong Coal Transport Harbor
2. 广东蛇口港码头
   Guangdong Shekou Harbor

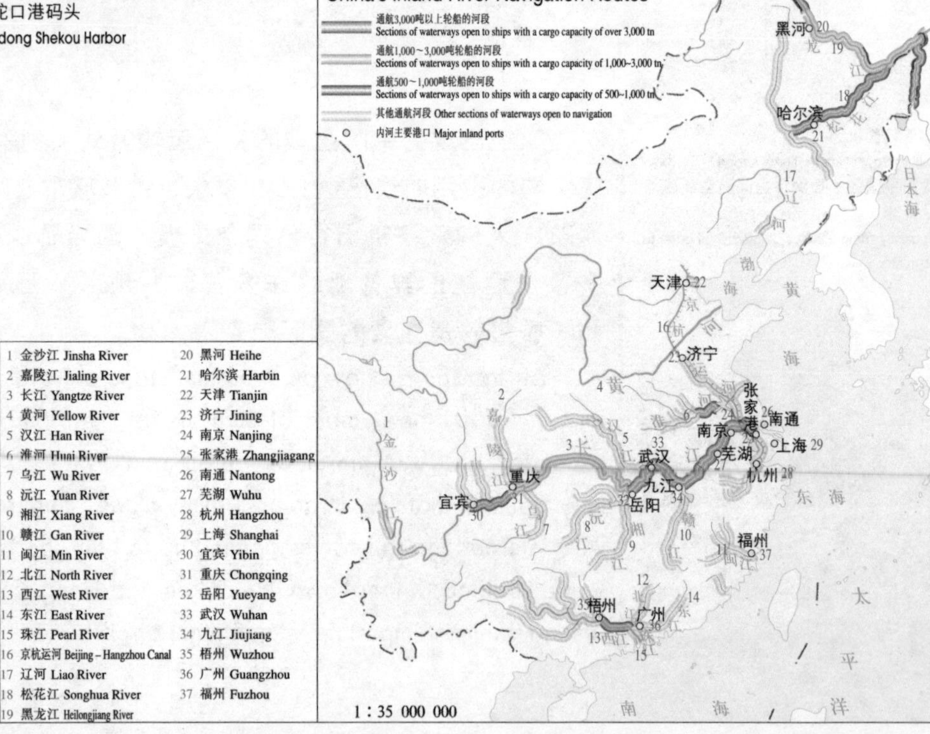

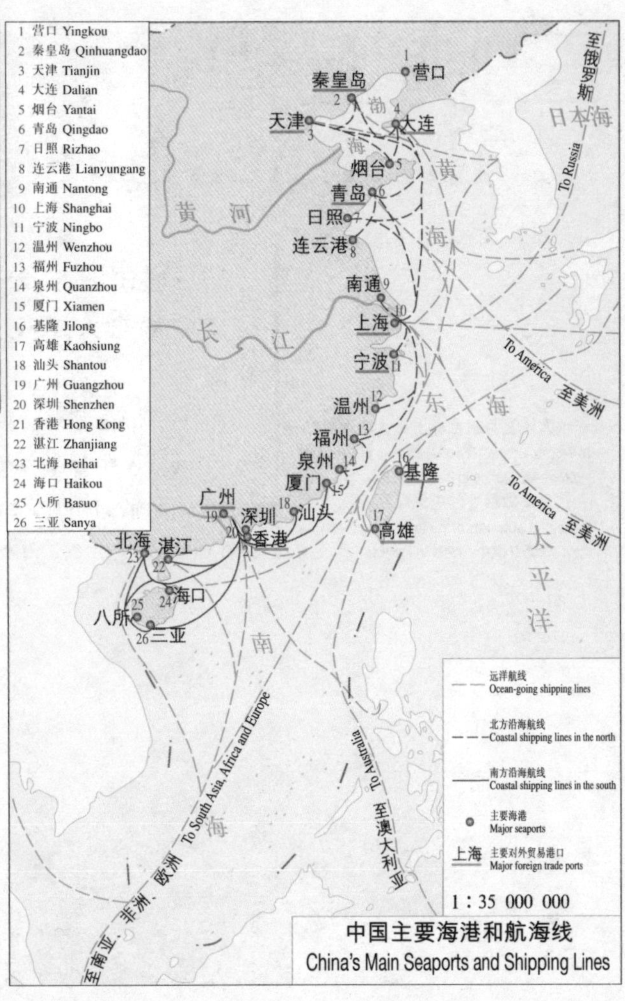

中国主要海港和航海线
China's Main Seaports and Shipping Lines

中国河流众多，海岸线漫长，水运条件优越。长江是中国最重要的内河航运大动脉。其干流从四川宜宾到入海口，全长2,813千米，全年可以通航，重庆、武汉、南京是长江沿岸重要的港口城市。珠江、松花江、黑龙江、淮河以及京杭运河也有一定的通航价值。

中国海运条件优越，拥有许多港口，如上海、大连、秦皇岛、天津、青岛、宁波、厦门、广州等。远洋船舶可达世界150多个国家和地区。

China has numerous rivers and a long coastline and advantageous water transport conditions. The Yangtze River is the most important inland shipping artery. Its main stream, from Yibin in Sichuan Province to the sea, has a total length of 2,813 km and is open to navigation all year round. Chongqing, Wuhan and Nanjing are important ports along the river. The Pearl River, the Songhua River, the Heilongjiang River, the Huaihe River and the Beijing-Hangzhou Canal are also of certain navigation value.

China has favorable conditions for marine transportation with many harbors, such as Shanghai, Dalian, Qinhuangdao, Tianjin, Qingdao, Ningbo, Xiamen, Guangzhou and so on. There are shipping routes from these ports to more than 150 countries and regions all over the world.

三峡工程
The Three Gorges Project

三峡工程，是一项综合治理长江和开发长江水能资源的宏大工程，具有防洪、发电、航运等综合功能。

The Three Gorges Project is a grand project to control the Yangtze River and exploit its hydropower potential. It has comprehensive functions of preventing floods, generating electricity and allowing passage of much larger ships than before.

1. 三峡大坝是目前世界上最大的水电站
The dam of the Three Gorges is the largest hydropower station in the world.
2. 世界上级数最多的内河船闸
The inland waterway of the Three Gorges has the most number of ship locks in the world.

三峡工程可以从根本上解除长江中下游的水患威胁。

三峡工程相当于10座200万千瓦的大型火力发电站，可以缓解华中和华东等地区的能源紧张状况。

三峡工程可以改善长江上游航道的通航条件。工程建成后，万吨级船队可以直达重庆，航运成本可降低35%，从而加强西南与其他地区的联系。

2

The Three Gorges Project can radically solve the flood threats of the middle and lower reaches of the Yangtze River.

It is equivalent to ten 2 million kw thermal power stations which can ease the problem of power shortages in central and eastern China, and other areas.

It can improve the navigational condition of the upper reaches of the Yangtze River. After its completion, 10,000–tn ships can reach Chongqing directly and 35% of the current shipping costs will be cut. The link between the southwest and other regions will be strengthened.

1

小资料 Data

三峡大坝高185米，电站装机总容量1,820万千瓦，年平均发电量约847亿千瓦时，是目前世界上最大的水电站。三峡工程1992年正式开工，总工期约18年，是一项跨世纪的工程。

The dam of the Three Gorges is 185 m high. The hydropower station has a capacity of 18.2 million kw. When its annual generating capability reaches 84.7 billion kw, it is the largest hydropower station in the world. The Three Gorges Project began in 1992 and was scheduled for completion in 18 years.

你知道吗 Do you know

长江三峡大坝是"世界第一坝"，坝长1,983米。它就像横跨长江的"水上长城"，是一处吸引游客的新景观。

The Three Gorges Dam of the Yangtze River is the biggest dam in the world. It is 1,983 m long. After its completion, it looks like a "Great Wall on the water", becoming a new landscape attracting tourists.

小浪底水利枢纽工程
The Xiaolangdi Key Water Control Project

小资料 Data

小浪底水利枢纽工程由一座坝长1,667米、最大坝高154米的斜心墙堆石坝、10座进水塔、9条泄洪排沙隧道、1条灌溉洞、6条引水发电洞和1座地下式厂房组成。

The Xiaolangdi Key Water Control Project is made up of a 1,667-m-long stone dam with a maximum height of 154 m, 10 intake towers, nine tunnels for flood and sand discharge, one irrigation cave, six caves for introducing water and generating electricity and one underground workshop.

你知道吗 Do you know

小浪底水利枢纽工程建成后，使黄河下游的防洪标准从现在的60年一遇提高到千年一遇。

After the completion of the Xiaolangdi Key Water Control Project, the standard of the flood control over the lower Yellow River will have been advanced from the former level of one major flood every 60 years to once in a thousand years.

小浪底位于河南洛阳以北40千米的黄河干流上，处在控制黄河下游泥沙的关键部位。小浪底水利枢纽工程是一座以防洪、减少泥沙淤积为主，兼顾灌溉、供水和发电等综合效益的特大型控制工程。

Xiaolangdi is located on the main stream of the Yellow River 40 km north of Luoyang in Henan Province and at the key point in terms of controlling the mud and sand content of the lower Yellow River. The Xiaolangdi Key Water Control Project is a comprehensive large-scale control project giving priority to controlling floods, reducing sand and mud deposits and also pays attention to irrigation, supplying water and generating electricity.

小浪底水库大坝
The dam of Xiaolangdi

南水北调
Water Diversion from South to North

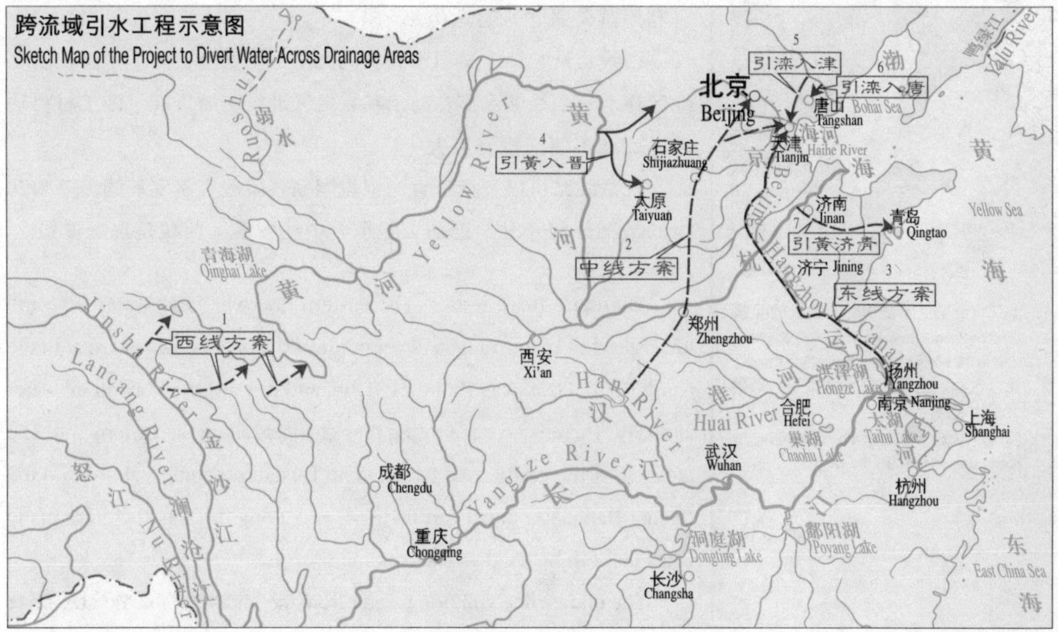

1	西线方案 Western Route Plan
2	中线方案 Middle Route Plan
3	东线方案 Eastern Route Plan
4	引黄入晋 Diversion of water from the Yellow River to Shanxi Province
5	引滦入津 Diversion of water from the Luanhe River to Tianjin
6	引滦入唐 Diversion of water from the Luanhe River to Tangshan
7	引黄济青 Diversion of water from the Yellow River to Jinan and Qingdao

中国的水资源，地区分布不均匀。总的来说南方多，北方少；东部多，西部少。随着人口的增加和经济的发展，北方缺水的情况日益严重，解决这一问题的办法之一就是跨流域调水，即南水北调。

Water resources in China are unevenly distributed. Generally speaking, the south is rich in water while the north is short of this commodity; the same applies to east and west. With the increase of population and rapid economic development, the problem of water shortage in the north is getting ever more serious. One solution is to divert water from one drainage area to another, namely, from south to north.

1. 长江水北调，可舒缓北方缺水的问题
Diverting Yangtze River water to north can bring relief to the water shortage in northern China.
2. 北方农村经常面对缺水的情况，影响农作物收成
The shortage of water in the northern region significantly affects the crop yield.

南水北调工程包括东、中、西三条线路。

东线：从长江下游提水，沿京杭运河北送，可为华北平原东部补水。渠长1,150千米，每年引水量300亿立方米。东线不需要开挖新干渠，可利用已建成的江都、淮安抽水站设施和京杭运河，并且沿途有许多湖泊可作为调节水库。

中线：从长江中游及其主要支流汉江引水到华北平原西部。全长1,000多千米，每年引水量300亿立方米，其优点是引水量大，还可利用落差兴建水力发电站。

西线：从长江上游引水到黄河上游，主要为黄河上中游及西北地区补水。西线调水都在高山峡谷地区进行，海拔高，施工材料缺乏，交通不便，投资巨大。

三条线路可以互相配合，根据国家各阶段经济发展的需要和财力的情况分期开发。近期实施东、中线方案，西线是远景设想。

There are three routes. The eastern line will carry water from the lower reaches of the Yangtze River northward along the Grand Canal to the North China Plain. It is about 1,150 km, and can divert 30 billion m^3 water annually. There is no need to dig new channels along the eastern line. The facilities of the established Jiangdu and Huaian pumping stations and the Beijing-Hangzhou Canal can be used, and along the way there are many lakes that can be used as reservoirs.

The middle line will bring water from the middle of the Yangtze River and its main tributary, the Han River, to the western side of the North China Plain. It is over 1,000 km long and could divert 30 billion m^3 of water annually. It can not only divert a large volume of water but also use the drop in altitude for hydropower.

The western line will divert water from the upper Yangtze River to the upper Yellow River to supply water for the upper and middle reaches of the latter and the northwestern regions. The western line will have to pass through mountains and gorges at high altitudes. Because of the lack of construction materials and inconvenient transportation, large investment is needed.

The three lines can be developed in stages according to need and the existing financial situation. For the moment, work is concentrated on the eastern and middle routes.

资源与环境 Resources and Environment

矿产资源
Mineral Resources

中国幅员辽阔，矿产资源丰富。已经探明的矿藏有145种，其中有些矿产为中国所独有。

China has a broad land and rich mineral resources. There are 145 confirmed minerals, some of which are only found in China.

1. 黑龙江双鸭山煤矿
   Mount Shuangya's coal mine, Heilongjiang
2. 新疆沙漠油井
   An oilfield in the desert of Xinjiang
3. 黑龙江大庆油田
   Daqing Oilfield, Heilongjiang
4. 北京首钢矿山采矿区
   Beijing's steel mine

煤炭作为中国的主要能源，其产量相当于世界煤炭总产量的30%，居世界第一位。主要有开滦、大同、阳泉、淮南等煤矿。

中国石油、天然气资源比较丰富。陆上油田主要分布在东北、华北、西北等地，如大庆、胜利、辽河、克拉玛依等油田。其中，大庆油田是中国最大的油田。正在大力勘探开发的塔里木盆地蕴藏着丰富的石油，有的地方已投入开采。此外，中国近海海域，也蕴藏着丰富的油气资源。

中国的铁矿储量约500亿吨，居世界前列。但是贫矿多，富矿少，矿石成分复杂。

中国的有色金属储量丰富，品种繁多，有“有色金属王国”之称。其中钨、锡、锑、锌、钛、锂等金属的储量居世界首位。

从矿产资源总量上看，中国是资源大国。但因中国人口众多，人均资源占有量不及世界平均水平的一半。

The output of the main energy resource in China, coal, amounts to 30% of the world's total. The chief coal mines are Kailuan, Datong, Yangquan and Huainan.

China is rich in oil and natural gas. Oilfields on land are distributed in Northeast, North and Northwest China, etc, such as Daqing, Shengli, Liaohe and Karamay oilfields. Among them, the Daqing Oilfield is the biggest oilfield in China. The Tarim Basin under development contains rich oil reserves. Some areas of the basin have been exploited. Apart from those, the offshore area is also rich in oil and natural gas.

China has approximate 50 billion tn of iron ore reserves, making it one of the few countries with rich iron ore resources. But most are low-grade iron ores whose composition is very complicated.

China abounds in nonferrous metals of great variety, giving it a reputation as the "kingdom of nonferrous metals". The reserves of tungsten, tin, stibium, zinc, titanium, lithium and so on are on top the world.

Calculated by total reserves, China is a big country with rich resources. But, because of the large population, the reserve per capita is less than half of that of the world.

动物资源
Animal Resources

中国的动物资源非常丰富，种类特别多，约占全世界动物种类的10％。其中鸟类1,175种，兽类414种，两栖类196种，爬行类315种，鱼类2,000多种。

有多种动物为中国所特有或主要分布在中国，如金丝猴、梅花鹿、丹顶鹤、大熊猫、扬子鳄、大鲵、野生双峰驼等。它们既是宝贵的自然资源，又是很有价值的旅游资源。

China has a great diversity of animals, with 10% of the world total. Among them are 1,175 birds, 414 beasts, 196 amphibious animals, 315 reptiles and over 2,000 species of fish.

Wild animals that can be only found or mainly distributed in China include golden-haired monkey, spotted deer, red-crowned crane, giant panda, Chinese alligator, giant salamander and wild two-humped camel. They are not only precious natural resources, but also valuable tourist resources.

丹顶鹤

丹顶鹤的寿命一般可达50～60年，所以又叫仙鹤。它体形优美，举止优雅，是著名的观赏鸟，主要以鱼、虫、水草为食，夏季生活在黑龙江省的沼泽地，冬季飞往南方越冬。

东北虎

东北虎，身体长约1.6～2米，是世界上体型最大的虎。它的前额上有似“王”字的斑纹，一般在夜间活动。主要分布在中国的东北地区，是国家一类保护动物。

麋鹿

麋鹿是中国特有的珍稀动物，因为它的角像鹿又不是鹿，头像马又不是马，身体像驴又不是驴，蹄子像牛又不是牛，所以又叫它“四不像”。因为它体形奇特，性情温驯，又非常稀少，是珍贵的观赏动物。

金丝猴

金丝猴是中国特有的珍贵动物，毛色金黄，非常光亮，像金丝一样，所以叫金丝猴。它们喜欢群居。

大熊猫

大熊猫是世界珍稀动物，毛色美观，性情温驯，动作笨拙，非常逗人喜爱。中国曾经把大熊猫当作国礼送给友好国家，它成了“和平、友谊的使者”。现在世界野生生物基金会用大熊猫的图案作为该组织的标徽。

扬子鳄

扬子鳄是珍稀的淡水鳄类之一，是中国的特有品种，因产于扬子江而得名。一般体长两米多，头、躯干扁平，皮肤上覆盖着大的鳞片，背面呈棕色，主要分布在安徽的宣城、广德、南陵等地。宣城建有扬子鳄自然保护区。

中国十分珍惜这些珍奇的野生动物，为了保护它们的生存环境，建立了许多自然保护区，如四川的卧龙自然保护区、云南的西双版纳自然保护区、湖北的神农架自然保护区等，并且成立了专门的保护机构。

The Red-Crowned Crane

The red-crowned crane can live for 50-60 years, therefore it is also known as the immortal crane. It has a graceful shape and elegant behavior that makes it a favorite for sightseeing. They live on fishes, insects and aquatic plants. In summer, they live in the swamps of Heilongjiang Province while in winter they fly south.

The Manchurian Tiger

Manchurian tigers, about 1.6 – 2 m long, are the largest tigers in the world. The patterns on its forehead resemble the Chinese character "wang," meaning the king. They move around at night. They mainly live in the northeast of China and are granted State first-grade protection.

David's Deer

David's deer are rare animals only found in China. It has horns like a deer, but it is not deer; its head is like a horse, but it is not horse; its body is like a donkey, but it's not donkey; and its hoof is like a cow's, but it's not cow, so it is called the "four-unlikeness". It is a rare animal for viewing because of its peculiar shape, tame temperament and small numbers.

Golden–Haired Monkey

Golden–haired monkeys are rare animals, their name coming from their shiny golden hair. They like living in groups.

Giant Panda

Giant pandas are rare animals in the world, with beautiful fur, calm temperament and clumsy movements. They are adorable. China has sent some as State presents to friendly countries. They have become "envoys of peace and friendship". Now the World Wildlife Fund (WWF) uses the panda as its logo.

Chinese Alligator (Yangtze Alligator)

The Chinese alligator is one of the rare freshwater alligators, which is peculiar to China. It is called Yangtze alligator in China because of its original habitat in the river. It is usually more than two meters long. Its head and body are flat and it is covered with big squamas. Its back is brown. They are mainly distributed in Xuancheng, Guangde and Nanling of Anhui Province. There is a natural reserve of Chinese alligators in Xuancheng.

China treasures these rare wild animals and protects their living environment. It has built many natural reserves, such as the Wolong Nature Reserve in Sichuan, the Xishuangbanna Nature Reserve in Yunnan, the Shennongjia Nature Reserve in Hubei and so on. And special protective bodies have been established.

植物资源 Plant Resources

中国地理环境复杂，植物种类丰富多样。据统计，高等植物共3万多种，占世界植物种类的1/10左右，其中有50多种珍贵植物为中国所特有。

China has a complicated geographical environment with a variety of plants. According to statistics, there are more than 30,000 species of higher plants, one-tenth of the world's total, and among them are over 50 species peculiar to China.

1. 原始森林中的老树
   The trees in virgin forest
2. 桦树林
   Red maples
3. 水杉
   Metasequoia

在众多的植物种类中，有各种各样的松树、终年常绿的柏树、姿态优美的杉树、清秀挺拔的竹子以及色彩缤纷的花卉等。

Among the plant species, there are various pine trees, evergreen cypresses, graceful China firs, delicate, tall and straight bamboos and colorful flowers, etc.

你知道吗 Do you know

闻名世界的三大"活化石"植物是水杉、银杏和银杉，它们在中国都有分布。

The three world-renowned "living fossil" plants are metasequoia, gingko and *Cathaya argyrophylla*. They all can be found in China.

水资源
Water Resources

中国水资源总量位居世界前列。但人均拥有量却低于许多国家，仅相当于世界人均占有量的1/4。

The total amount of water resources in China leads the world. But water per capita is only a quarter of the world average.

中国江河湖泊众多，主要河流有长江、黄河、珠江、雅鲁藏布江、松花江等；主要湖泊有洞庭湖、鄱阳湖、洪泽湖、太湖、巢湖等。另外，冰川面积也比较大，是重要的淡水资源。

中国水资源地区分布不均匀。总的来说是东南多，西北少，由东南向西北递减。

China abounds in rivers and lakes. The main ones are the Yangtze River, Yellow River, Pearl River, Yarlung Zangbo River and Songhua River, in terms of freshwater lakes, the main ones already mentioned are Dongting Lake, Poyang Lake, Hongze Lake, Taihu Lake and Chaohu Lake. In addition, there is a large area of glaciers that are an important freshwater source.

China's water resources are unevenly distributed. General speaking, there is much more water in southeast than in northwest. The water resources descend from southeast to northwest.

环境保护
Environmental Protection

中国是一个发展中的大国，又处在工业化的过程中，环境问题比较突出，因此国家把环境保护列为一项基本国策。

China is a big developing country and in the process of industrialization; therefore, the environmental problem is comparatively prominent. The government has consequently taken environmental protection as one of the basic national policies.

吉林长白山自然保护区
Mount Changbai Nature Reserve, Jilin

1. 四川卧龙自然保护区
   Wolong Nature Reserve, Sichuan
2. "三北"(东北、华北、西北)防护林工程
   The shelter-forests project in Northern, Northeastern and Northwestern China

近年来，中国政府采取了各种措施来加强环境治理，如建立了世界著名的生态工程"三北防护林工程"，大力发展和广泛建立自然保护区，颁布了《环境保护法》，加强环境保护的宣传和教育。目前，环境治理已取得了明显成效，大部分城市环境和农业生态环境得到了改善，工业污染防治能力也大大提高，环境保护已成为人人关心的话题，日益得到人们的重视。

It has taken various measures to strengthen environmental improvement in recent years, such as the world famous ecological project "the shelter-forests in Northern, Northwestern and Northeastern China". In addition, nature reserves have been greatly developed. The Law on Environmental Protection has been enacted and education on environmental protection issues has been greatly strengthened. Now, great achievements have been gained in environmental improvement. The environment in most cities and the agricultural ecological environment have much improved. The capability of preventing and controlling industrial pollution has been greatly expanded. Environmental protection has become a topic of concern to all.

小资料 Data

中国政府强化环境污染的综合治理。到2005年，城市污水集中处理率要达到45%；重点地区二氧化硫排放量比2000年减少20%；开展全民环保教育，提高全民环保意识，推行绿色消费方式。

The Chinese government has strengthened the comprehensive control over the environmental pollution. By 2005, the rate of the centralized sewage disposal will reach 45%; the amount of sulfur dioxide discharge in key areas will decrease by 20% compared to that of 2000. National environmental protection education has been advocated, awareness of civil involvement in environmental protection has been enhanced, and green consumption methods have been promoted.

历史名城与现代都市
Famous Historical Cities and Modern Cities

北　京
Beijing

北京是中华人民共和国的首都，是全国的政治、文化和科技教育的中心，也是全国的交通和国际交往中心。

Beijing is the capital of the People's Republic of China, the center of politics, culture and scientific education of the state and also the center of transportation and international exchange.

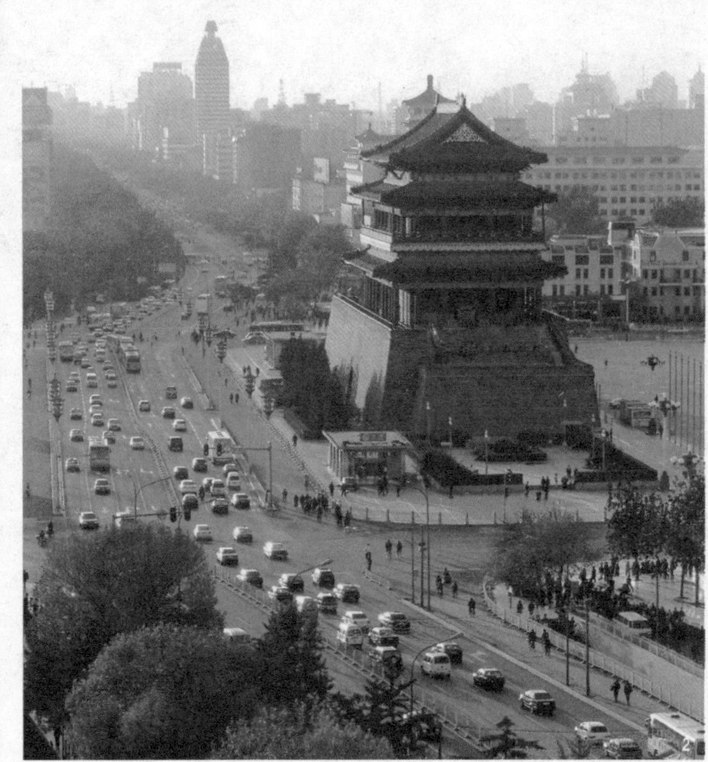

1. 故宫全貌
   A panoramic view of the Palace Museum
2. 北京市容
   Beijing City

中华人民共和国成立50多年来，首都北京的建设日新月异，发生了翻天覆地的变化。现代化建筑如雨后春笋般相继崛起，高楼大厦鳞次栉比。2008年奥运会将在北京举行，这将大大推进城市的建设与改造，到那时，北京将以更新的面貌展现在世人面前。

北京科技力量强大，有中国科学院、北京大学、清华大学等世界著名科研机构和高等学府。同时，北京正大力发展高新技术产业，如人才密集的中关村，被称为中国的"硅谷"。

北京作为闻名中外的历史文化名城，正在建设成为一座既有古典魅力，又有现代风采的国际化大都市。

小资料 Data

故宫建成至今已有500多年的历史，占地总面积约72万平方米，四周有10米多高的城墙，城墙外有宽50多米的护城河环绕。

The Palace Museum has a history of over 500 years. Covering an area of about 720,000 m², it is encircled with walls more than 10 m tall, beyond which flows a 50 m wide moat.

天安门

1949年10月1日，天安门广场举行了盛大的开国大典，升起了第一面五星红旗。毛泽东主席站在天安门城楼上庄严地宣告"中华人民共和国成立了"。

2

3

人民英雄纪念碑

人民英雄纪念碑耸立在天安门广场中央，碑的正面是毛泽东主席的题词“人民英雄永垂不朽”，背面是周恩来总理题写的碑文。纪念碑共用17,000多块花岗岩和汉白玉砌成，雄伟壮观。

故宫

故宫又称紫禁城，是明、清两朝的皇宫。1987年被联合国列入世界文化遗产名录。

故宫是世界上最大的皇家宫殿群，内有宫室9,000多间，主要分为“前朝”和“内廷”两部分。前朝以太和殿、中和殿、保和殿为中心，内廷由乾清宫、交泰殿、坤宁宫、御花园及两侧的东、西六宫组成。

故宫是中国最大的国家博物馆，也是最丰富的文化和艺术宝库。宫内藏有大量的历史文物和历代艺术珍品。它的独特建筑风格，是中国古代建筑的精华。

太和殿是皇帝举行大典的地方，高35米，是中国最大、最富丽堂皇的殿堂。殿内的雕龙宝座是金漆的，柱子则是沥金粉漆的。地上的方砖能敲出金石的声音，称为金砖，因此，太和殿又被称为金銮殿。

颐和园

颐和园是万寿山和昆明湖的总称，是中国目前最大的古代园林，现已被联合国列入世界文化遗产名录。

颐和园内有山有水，整体构思巧妙，是世界上罕见的园林杰作。佛香阁是颐和园的中心建筑和标志，气势雄伟，在这里可以看到全园的景色。

颐和园长廊，始建于乾隆十五年（1750年），全长728米，共有273间，中间建有象征春、夏、秋、冬的四座重檐八角亭。

长廊上技艺独特的中国绘画，把中华民族追求美的情趣，淋漓尽致地表现出来。

1. 建设日新月异的北京城
   The modern Beijing City
2. 人民英雄纪念碑
   Monument to the People's Heroes
3. 乾清宫的皇帝宝座
   The imperial throne in the Hall of Celestial Purity

 小资料 Data

天坛分为内坛和外坛两部分，主要建筑物都在内坛。

The Temple of Heaven can be divided into two parts: inner altar and outer altar. The main buildings are in the inner altar.

天坛

天坛建于1420年，是明、清两代皇帝每年祭天和祈祷五谷丰收的地方。天坛建筑结构奇特，装饰精美，在世界上享有极高的声誉，现已被联合国列入世界文化遗产名录。

In the 50-odd years after the founding of the PRC, the capital has developed quickly and adopted a new look. Modern buildings rise up one by one like bamboo shoots in spring after rain, with row upon row of skyscrapers soaring into the sky. In 2008, the Summer Olympic Games will be held in Beijing, which will promote the construction and renovation of this city greatly. At that time, Beijing will take on an even newer look before the world.

Beijing has strong force engaged in science. The Chinese Academy of Sciences, Peking University and Tsinghua University are among the world famous scientific research bodies and institutions of higher learning. At the same time, Beijing is making efforts to develop new advanced technology fields, such as in the Zhongguancun area, now called "Silicon Valley".

As a world-renowned city of history and culture, Beijing is being developed into an international metropolis of classical charm and modern charisma.

1. 天坛祈年殿
   The Hall of Prayer for Good Harvests
2. 颐和园
   The Summer Palace
3. 太和殿藻井
   The caisson ceiling of the Hall of Supreme Harmony

1

2

Tiananmen Square

On October 1, 1949, the founding ceremony of PRC was held on Tiananmen Square, and the first five-star red flag was raised. Chairman Mao Zedong stood on Tiananmen gate and declared solemnly, "The People's Republic of China is founded!"

Monument to the People's Heroes

The Monument to the People's Heroes stands in the middle of Tiananmen Square. On its front is the inscription from Chairman Mao Zedong that "Eternal Glory to the People's Heroes"; on its back is an epigraph written by Premier Zhou Enlai. The monument is made of 17,000 pieces of granite and white marbles, and it looks majestic and spectacular.

The Palace Museum

The Palace Museum, also named the Forbidden City, was the royal palace of the Ming and Qing dynasties. In 1987, it was put into the list of world cultural heritage sites by UNESCO.

The Palace Museum is the world's largest royal palace complex, and there are more than 9,000 rooms divided into two parts: "front court" and "inner court". The front court is centered on the Hall of Supreme Harmony, Hall of Central Harmony and Hall of Preserved Harmony. The inner court is

你知道吗 Do you know

3

皇帝的宝座上方有个藻井，藻井中央有条浮雕蟠龙，龙嘴里衔着一颗铜胎水银球。这个球叫轩辕球，挂在宝座上方是为了显示皇帝是轩辕氏的子孙，是正统继承者。

Over the imperial throne is a caisson ceiling. In the middle of it there is a coiled dragon in relief holding a mercury-gilded bronze ball in its mouth. The ball is called Xuanyuan (surname of the Yellow Emperor, legendary first Chinese ancestor), which is hung over the imperial throne to show that the emperor is the offspring of the Xuanyuan Family, and, therefore, a legitimate successor.

1

 你知道吗 Do you know

颐和园原是元朝和明朝皇帝的行宫花园，在清朝乾隆年间，改建为清漪园。1860年被英法联军烧毁，1888年，慈禧太后不顾国家民族安危，挪用海军经费3,000万两白银来重建这座花园，并改名为颐和园。

The Summer Palace was the garden of the temporary dwelling place for emperors of the Yuan and Ming dynasties for short stays when they were away from the Forbidden City. During the reign of Emperor Qianlong in the Qing Dynasty, it was reconstructed into the Garden of Clear Ripples. In 1860, it was burnt down by British and French forces. In 1888, it was reconstructed on orders of Empress Dowager Cixi with funds meant for the navy, regardless of the nation's safety, and it was renamed the Garden of Harmonious Nature.

made up of the Hall of Celestial Purity, Hall of Celestial and Terrestrial Union, Palace of Terrestrial Tranquility, the Imperial Garden and six palaces at the eastern and western sides.

The Palace Museum is the biggest national museum in China with the richest cultural and artistic treasures. In it are kept an abundance of historical, cultural relics and artistic treasures of every dynasty. Its unique architectural style is the essence of Chinese classical architecture.

The Hall of Supreme Harmony is a place where emperors held important ceremonies. It is about 35 m tall and the largest and most magnificent hall in China. The precious throne is carved with gilded dragons, and the columns are also gilded. The square bricks can make a sound like metal, therefore, the Hall of Supreme Harmony is also called the Hall of Golden Chimes.

The Summer Palace (The Garden of Harmonious Nature)

The Garden of Harmonious Nature (known as the Summer Palace in the West) is a general name for the Hill of Longevity and Kunming Lake. It is the largest classical garden in China and has listed by UNESCO as a world cultural heritage site.

There are mountains and lakes in the Summer Palace. It has an ingenious layout and is a rare masterpiece among the gardens of the world. The Pagoda of Buddhist Incense is the main building and an emblem of the Summer Palace. Standing on the majestic pagoda, one can have a panoramic view of the garden.

The long corridor of the Summer Palace was first built in the 15th year of the reign of Emperor Qianlong in the Qing Dynasty (1750 AD). It is 728 m long with 273 bays, including four double-eaved octagonal pavilions symbolizing the four seasons of the year.

Chinese paintings along the corridor show the Chinese people's love for beauty incisively and vividly.

The Temple of Heaven

The Temple of Heaven was built in 1420, and was where emperors of the Ming and Qing dynasties offered sacrifices to heaven and prayed for a good harvest. Enjoying high reputation in the world, it has special architecture and delicate decorations and is now listed by UNESCO as a world cultural heritage site.

1. 故宫博物院神武门
The Gate of Divine Military Genius (Shenwumen) within the Palace Museum
2. 北京近年大力推进城市的建设与改造，面貌一新
Beijing has been undergoing dramatic changes in city planning and rezoning in recent years.

2

上　海
Shanghai

上海位于长江入海口，是中国最大的城市，同时也是一座历史文化名城和著名的旅游城市。

上海是中国最大的经济中心，是全国最重要的工业基地，也是重要的贸易、金融和文化中心。上海港是世界第三大港。

Located on the estuary of the Yangtze River, Shanghai is not only the largest city but also a famous city of history, culture and tourism. It is the biggest economic center and the most important industrial base in China. It is also an important center of trade, finance and culture and the third biggest port in the world.

1. 上海是中国最大的城市，也是一座历史文化名城。图中对岸是东方明珠电视塔
Not only is Shanghai the largest city of China, but also a famous city of history, culture and tourism. The building in the center of the picture is the Oriental Pearl TV Tower.
2. 往来浦东国际机场与浦西市中心之间的快速磁悬浮列车
Shanghai's Magnetic Levitation Train links Pudong Internation Airport to downtown Puxi.

东方明珠电视塔

东方明珠电视塔，矗立在黄浦江边，塔高468米，是目前世界第三、亚洲第一高塔。

外滩

外滩是上海最著名的旅游景点之一。外滩建筑风格多样，有古代的，现代的，有中国的和外国的，享有“万国建筑博览会”之美誉。

杨浦大桥

建在黄浦江上的杨浦大桥，是目前世界上跨度最大的双塔双索斜拉桥，全长7,654米，主桥长1,172米，中孔跨度602米，引桥全长6,480米，主塔高208米，呈倒“Y”形。

1. 上海夜景
   Shanghai at night
2. 杨浦大桥
   Yangpu Bridge

豫园

豫园位于上海市黄浦区，占地两万多平方米，是著名的江南古典园林。

豫园围墙上缀有五条巨龙，龙身用瓦片砌成。五条巨龙形态各异，非常好看。

Oriental Pearl TV Tower

The Oriental Pearl TV Tower, by the Huangpu River, is 468 m high. It is the third tallest tower in the world and the tallest in Asia.

The "Bund"

The "bund" is the most famous scenic spot in Shanghai where there are various styles of construction, including classical and modern, domestic and foreign, earning it the nickname of "architectural exposition of many countries".

小知识 Knowledge

上海市人口约1,674万。气候温暖湿润，四季分明。

Shanghai has a population of 16.74 million. It has warm and moist climate with clear differences between the four seasons.

2

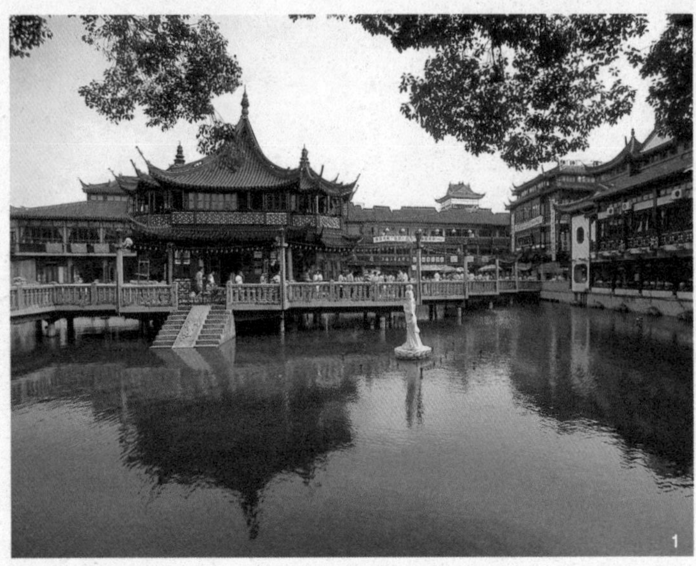

Yangpu Bridge

Built over the Huangpu River, the Yangpu Bridge is a double-tower, double-chain stayed-cable bridge with the longest span in the world. It is about 7,654 m long with a 1,172 m main span. The middle arch spans over 602 m, the bridge approaches are about 6,480 m long and the main tower, which looks like an upside-down Y, is 208 m tall.

1. 上海豫园
   Yuyuan Garden, Shanghai
2. 豫园围墙上的巨龙
   The walls of Yuyuan Garden are decorated with huge dragons.

Yuyuan Garden

Yuyuan Garden, located in the Huangpu District, is a famous classical garden in Jiangnan (the area south of the Yangtze River), covering an area of over 20,000 m^2.

Its walls are decorated with five huge dragons made of tiles. Varied in shape and expressions, the five dragons look magnificent.

天 津
Tianjin

天津市容
A bird's-eye view of Tianjin

天津市位于华北平原的东北部，东临渤海，背靠燕山，是中国北方的经济中心，是首都北京的海上门户。天津是现代工业中心之一。

Located in the northeast of the North China Plain, bordering the Bohai Sea and lying against Yanshan Mountain, Tianjin is the economic center of north China and Beijing's outlet to the sea. It is also one of the country's modern industrial centers.

1. 水上公园
Park on Water
2. 独乐寺
Monastery of Solitary Pleasure
3. 盘山挂月峰
Guayue Peak, Mt. Panshan

天津的“泥人张”彩塑、杨柳青年画、“魏记”风筝、“刻砖刘”四大民间艺术，驰名天下。

水上公园

水上公园是天津市最大的公园。全园以水取胜，水面占公园总面积的3/5，故名“水上公园”。园中有岛屿、湖泊，亭、台、楼、阁点缀其间，具有江南水乡特色。

独乐寺

独乐寺又称大佛寺，始建于唐代。主要建筑是山门和观音阁。

盘山

盘山位于天津市蓟县西北部，平均海拔500米，山青水秀，被誉为“京东第一山”，是天津著名的游览胜地之一。

The four great folk arts—"Clay Man Zhang" painted sculpture, New Year's paintings of Yangliuqing, "Wei Family" kites and "Carved Bricks Liu"—are famous at home and abroad.

Park on Water

The Park on Water is the biggest park in Tianjin. Most of the attractions are based on water, which covers 60% of the total area. The park is full of islets, lakes, pavilions, terraces, buildings and towers with characteristics of water villages in southeast China.

Monastery of Solitary Pleasure

The Monastery of Solitary Pleasure, also called the Monastery of the Great Buddha, was first built in the Tang Dynasty. The main buildings are the mountain gate and the Avalokitesvara Building.

2

Mt. Panshan

Located in the northwest of Jixian County of Tianjin, with an average altitude of 500 m, Mt. Panshan has green mountains and clear water. It is honored as "the best mountain to the east of Beijing" and one of the famous tourist spots in Tianjin.

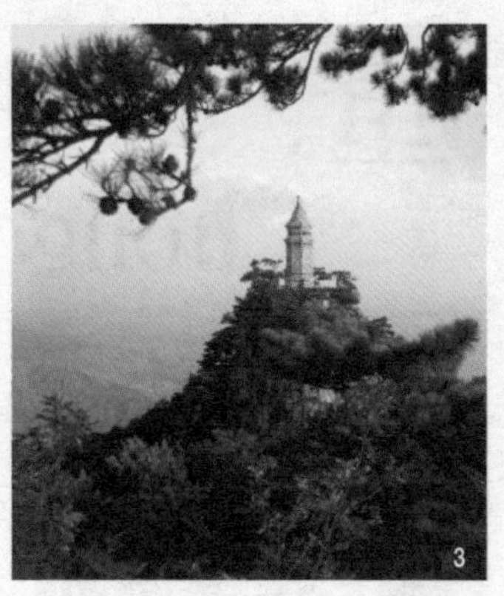
3

小资料 Data

天津有现代化的深水海港，天津新港是中国目前最大的人工海港之一。

Tianjin has modern deep-water harbors. Tianjin New Harbor is one of the biggest man-made harbors in China.

观音阁是中国现存最古老的木结构高层楼阁。1976年唐山大地震时，观音阁顶部晃动幅度达1～2米。地震后，它又恢复原状，稳如泰山。观音阁内观音立像高16米，头顶上有10个小佛头，所以又叫十一面观音。

The Avalokitesvara Building is the oldest existing high-rise wooden tower in China. In the Tangshan Earthquake in 1976, the top swayed a distance of one to two meters, but it remained as stable as Mt. Tai. In it, there is a 16-m-tall statue of Avalokitesvara over whose head there are ten small Buddha heads, earning it the name of 11-faced Avalokitesvara.

重　庆
Chongqing

你知道吗 Do you know

北京、上海、天津、重庆是属于中央人民政府直接管辖的直辖市。

Beijing, Shanghai, Tianjin and Chongqing are municipalities directly under the Central Government.

重庆位于四川盆地的东南部。老城区一面靠山，三面临江，形状像半岛。市内丘陵起伏，有“山城”之美名。

Chongqing is located in the southeast of the Sichuan Basin. The old city lies against mountains on one side and is bordered by rivers on the other three sides, looking like a peninsular. It is a city perched on undulating hills.

重庆在四川盆地内，降水多，湿度大。冬季多雾，所以有“雾都”之称；夏季特别炎热，是长江沿岸“三大火炉”城市之最。

重庆风光迷人，特别是夜景非常著名。市内有北温泉公园、南温泉公园，郊县有大足石刻等名胜古迹。

小资料 Data

重庆市是中国西南最大的工商业中心和长江上游水陆交通枢纽及经济中心。

Chongqing is the biggest industrial and commercial center in southwestern China and the hub of water and land transportation and the economic center of the upper Yangtze River region.

北温泉公园

北温泉公园位于嘉陵江畔，依山傍水，风景优美，园内景色以明朝时重建的四大殿为中心。东边的古香园中古木参天，是游人休息的好去处；石刻园内有用整石雕刻而成的盘龙塔，高2米，为珍贵的明代文物。园内还有迂回曲折的溶洞，并设有温泉游泳池。

大足石刻

大足石刻造像建于唐宋时期，数量多达五万余尊，造像的造型千姿百态，各具特色，为中国石像中所罕见，现已被联合国列入世界文化遗产名录。

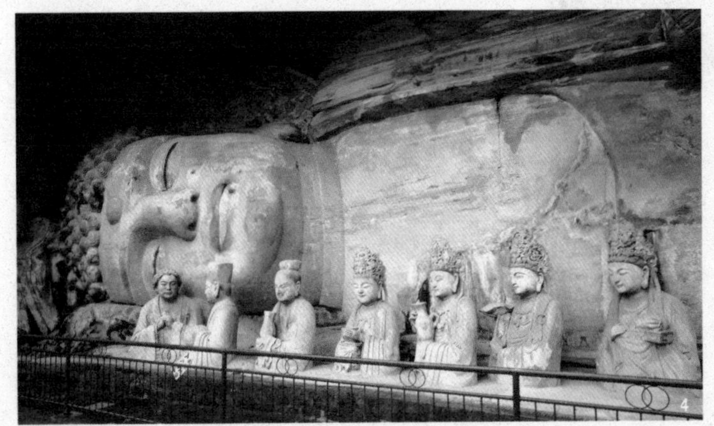

1. 重庆山城
   Chongqing City lies against mountains on one side.
2. 重庆人民大礼堂
   The People's Auditorium in Chongqing
3. 解放碑是重庆市中心商业区
   The Liberation Monument is located in the center of Chongqing's commercial district.
4. 大足石刻
   Dazu Stone Carvings

1. 重庆山城夜景
Chongqing at night
2. 重庆北温泉公园
Chongqing Northern Hot Spring Park

Located in the Sichuan Basin, Chongqing has plenty of rain and high humidity. In winter, it is mostly foggy, while in summer it becomes one of the three "hot-like-a-stove" cities along the Yangtze River.

Chongqing has attractive scenery, especially at night. In the downtown area, there are the northern and southern hot spring parks, and there are many famous scenic spots and historic sites on the outskirts, such as the Dazu Stone Carvings, etc.

Northern Hot Spring Park

Located on the bank of the Jialing River, the Northern Hot Spring Park lies against mountains and water with beautiful scenery. The park takes the four halls rebuilt in the Ming Dynasty as the center. Old trees tower into the sky in the Garden of Classical Fragrance east of the park, which is a good place for tourists to have a rest; in the Garden of Stone Carvings there is a cultural relic of the Ming Dynasty, the two-meter-tall Tower of Coiled Dragon which was carved out of rock. There are also winding caves with hot spring swimming pools.

考考你 Do you know

你知道中国长江沿岸"三大火炉"城市的名称吗？(重庆、武汉、南京)

Do you know the names of the three "hot-like-a-stove" cities along the Yangtze River? (Chongqing, Wuhan, Nanjing)

The Dazu Stone Carvings

The sculptures of the Dazu Stone Carvings were created during the Tang and Song dynasties. There are more than 50,000 statues, varied in gestures and expressions, which are very rare among Chinese stone statues; UNESCO lists them as world cultural relics.

南京 Nanjing

南京是江苏省的省会，也是中国七大古都之一。它风景优美，名胜古迹众多，是中国历史文化名城。其水、陆、空交通发达，是江苏省最大的综合性工业城市。

Nanjing is the capital city of Jiangsu Province, and also one of the seven ancient cities in China. It has beautiful scenery and many famous scenic spots and historic sites. It has developed water, land and air transportation links, and is the biggest comprehensive industrial city in Jiangsu Province.

1. 明代兴建的中华门，距今有6百多年历史
   Built in Ming Dynasty (1368-1644 AD), the China Gate has more than 600 years of history.
2. 中山陵是孙中山先生的陵墓
   Sun Yat-sen Mausoleum

小资料 Data

历史上，曾经先后有吴、东晋、宋、齐、梁、陈等6个朝代在南京建都，所以称它为“六朝古都”。后来，明朝初和太平天国也曾在此建都。

In history, there were six dynasties of Wu, Eastern Jin, Song, Qi, Liang and Chen, which successively chose Nanjing as their capital. Later on, the early Ming Dynasty and the Taiping Heavenly Kingdom (1851 – 1864 AD) also settled in the city.

中华门

中华门是南京城墙的最大城门，由三道瓮城和四道城门组成，南北长128米，东西宽118.5米，总面积达15,168平方米。城墙高21.45米，工程宏伟，结构复杂，设计巧妙，在中国城墙建筑史上占有极其重要的地位。

中山陵

中山陵是中国伟大的民主革命先行者孙中山先生的陵墓。陵墓像一个大钟，由南往北沿山势逐渐升高，共有392级台阶。整个建筑群布局严整，庄严雄伟，被誉为“中国近代建筑史上的第一陵”。

孙中山先生浩气长存，永远为世人所敬仰。

秦淮河

秦淮河是著名的游览胜地，分为内河和外河。内河在南京城内，是十里秦淮最繁华的地方。秦淮风光最著名的是自明代沿袭至今的灯船。河上的船，不论大小，一律悬挂着彩灯。到秦淮河游玩的人，都以乘灯船为乐事。

夫子庙

夫子庙位于秦淮河北岸，始建于公元1034年，原是供奉和祭祀孔子的地方，现已成为群众文化活动场所。夫子庙古建筑群，包括周围的茶馆、酒楼、店铺等建筑都是明清风格。这里的传统食品和风味小吃非常多，品种不下200种。

1. 秦淮河
   Qinhuai River
2. 南京新街口夜市
   Xinjiekou night market, Nanjing
3. 南京长江大桥
   Yangtze Bridge, Nanjing

雨花台

雨花台是一个高约100米的山岗，上面有很多雨花石，形状像鹅蛋一样，色彩艳丽，惹人喜爱。中华人民共和国成立以后，为了纪念在此牺牲的共产党人和爱国人士，在这里修建了烈士陵园。

南京长江大桥

南京长江大桥是中国第一座自己设计建造的双层双线公路、铁路两用大桥。上层的公路桥长4,589米；下层的铁路桥长6,772米，铺有双轨，两列火车可同时对开。江面上的正桥长1,577米，正桥的桥孔跨度达160米，桥下可行万吨巨轮。整座大桥像一条彩虹凌空江上，十分壮观。它是中国造桥史上的一座里程碑，是中国人民的骄傲。

The China Gate

The China Gate is the biggest gate in the city wall of Nanjing, which is made up of three urn-like city walls and four gates. From south to north it is 128 m long and from east to west 118.5 m wide, covering an area of 15,168 m^2. The wall, 21.45 m high, is a magnificent project of complicated structure and fine design. It occupies a very important position in the history of China's city wall construction.

Sun Yat-sen Mausoleum

Sun Yat-sen is the great pioneer of the democratic revolution in China. His mausoleum, like a big bell, ascends from south to north and has 392 stairs. The whole building complex is designed to display a solemn and majestic air, and it is honored as "the best mausoleum in the history of China's modern architecture".

Mr. Sun Yat-sen's noble spirit will never perish and people will admire him forever.

Qinhuai River

The Qinhuai River, a famous scenic spot, is made up of the inner river and outer river. The inner river is in the city of Nanjing, which is the busiest place along the five-kilometer Qinhuai. The biggest attraction of Qinhuai is the lantern boats tracing back to the Ming Dynasty. All the boats on the river, big or small, have colorful lanterns hung up and everyone enjoys taking a ride on the boats.

Confucius Temple

Located on the northern bank of the Qinhuai River, the Confucius Temple was first built in 1034, and was originally a place for enshrining and offering sacrifice for Confucius. This ancient construction complex, including surrounding teahouses, restaurants and stores, were all built in the style of the Ming and Qing dynasties. There are more than 200 different traditional foods available today.

Terrace of Raining Flowers

The Terrace of Raining Flowers is about 100 m tall. On it, there are many colorful pebbles like goose eggs in various colors. After the founding of the PRC, to commemorate those communists and patriots who died for the revolution, a mausoleum of martyrs was built here.

The Great Yangtze River Bridge of Nanjing

The Great Yangtze River Bridge of Nanjing is the first double-decker and double-line dual-use bridge of road and railway designed by China itself. The road of the upper deck is 4,589 m long; the railway of the lower deck is 6,772 m long with double rails. The main bridge over the river is 1,577 m long, with an arch spanning some 160 m that allows passage of 10,000-tn ships. The whole bridge looks very splendid like a rainbow hanging over the river. It is a milestone in the Chinese history of bridge construction and a pride of Chinese people.

3

你知道吗 Do you know

二三百万年前，雨花台是一个低洼地。河水从上游冲来大量玛瑙卵石，后来地壳抬升，河滩变成高地，美丽的卵石便留在雨花台上了。

Two or three million years ago, the Terrace of Raining Flowers was a low-lying land. The flowing water brought a large number of agate pebbles from the upper reaches of the river. Later, the crust of the earth rose up and the low-lying land became upland with the beautiful pebbles remaining.

苏州 Suzhou

苏州位于江苏省南部，既是一座历史文化名城，又是一座经济发达的现代化都市，有着良好的投资环境，对外开放程度较高。苏州工业园区和苏州新区吸引了大量的外商投资，其高新技术产业发展迅速。

Suzhou, located in south of Jiangsu Province, is not only a famous historical and cultural city but also a modern city with a developed economy, excellent investment environment and high degree of opening up to the outside world. The industrialized area and the new area of Suzhou have attracted many foreign businessmen to invest. Its new and high-tech products develop very fast.

小资料 Data

苏州市交通发达，气候温暖湿润，物产丰富，是“鱼米之乡”。这里的丝绸更是举世闻名，有“丝绸之乡”的美誉。

Suzhou City has advanced transportation, warm and moist weather and rich products. The silk produced here is world famous.

苏州市内园林特别多，是著名的“园林之城”，有“江南园林甲天下，苏州园林甲江南”之说。城内小河纵横，小桥达380多座，有“东方威尼斯”之称。

1997年12月，苏州古典园林被联合国列入世界文化遗产名录。

苏州有四大名园：沧浪亭、狮子林、拙政园、留园。它们分别代表着宋、元、明、清四个朝代园林建筑的艺术风格。

沧浪亭

沧浪亭是苏州最古老的一所名园，为宋代诗人苏子美所筑。园内以假山为主，山上古木参天，著名的沧浪亭就隐蔽其中。

狮子林

狮子林是元代园林的代表。它以太湖石堆砌的假山精巧而著称，很多石峰形状像狮子，千姿百态，栩栩如生，因而得名。

拙政园

拙政园建于明朝，全园分为东园、中园、西园三部分。

中园是拙政园的精华部分，其总体布局以水池为中心，亭台楼榭临水而建，有的亭榭则直接从水中冒出来，具有江南水乡的特色。

留园

留园具有清代园林的风格。它以水池为中心：池南的涵碧山房与明瑟楼是其主体建筑；池北多为假山小亭，林木交映；池西假山上的闻木樨香轩，是俯视全园景色最佳处，并有长廊与各处相通；池东以曲院回廊见胜，有三座石峰，中间为冠云峰，高9米，是江南最大的太湖石。

There are many gardens in Suzhou, which is reputed to be “a city of gardens”. There is a saying about it that goes “gardens in area south of the Yangtze River are the best in the world, while gardens in Suzhou are the best in the area south of the Yangtze River”. The city is crisscrossed with streams and more than 380 bridges, creating a “Venice of the East”.

In December 1997, UNESCO listed the classical gardens of Suzhou as

1. 苏州城内小河纵横，有“东方威尼斯”之称
   Suzhou City is crisscrossed with streams and bridges, creating a “Venice of the East”.
2. 沧浪亭
   Canglang Garden
3. 狮子林
   Lion Garden
4. 拙政园
   The Humble Administrator's Garden

你知道吗 Do you know

拙政园、留园、北京的颐和园和承德避暑山庄称为中国四大古典名园。

The Humble Administrator's Garden, the Liu Garden, the Summer Palace in Beijing and the Summer Resort in Chengde are reputed to be the four famous classical gardens in China.

留园
Liu Garden

小故事 Anecdote

狮子林有个真趣亭。据说乾隆皇帝游玩狮子林后，挥笔题了"真有趣"三个字。有个新科状元觉得不雅，但又不能批评皇上，于是便说"臣见御笔的铁划银钩，其中这'有'字更是龙飞凤舞，望圣上将这'有'字赐给微臣。"皇上听懂了他的话意，便点头同意。"真有趣"便成了"真趣"。

There is the Pavilion of Natural Fun in the Lion Garden. It is said that after Emperor Qianlong (1736 – 1796 AD) visited the Lion Garden, he wrote three characters of "have natural fun". A newly-conferred Number One Scholar (title conferred on the person who came out first in the highest imperial examination) thought it was not very good, but he couldn't say so before the emperor, therefore he said, "Your vassal sees that your Majesty's calligraphy is forceful and elegant, especially the character 'have' is as beautiful as a flying dragon and dancing phoenix. I hope your Majesty could grant it as a gift to your humble vassal." The emperor understood what he meant, thus he nodded and "have natural fun" became "natural fun".

a world cultural heritage site.

There are four famous gardens in Suzhou: the Canglang Garden, Lion Garden, Humble Administrator's Garden and the Liu Garden. They represent the architectural styles of the Song, Yuan, Ming, Qing dynasties respectively.

Canglang Garden

The Canglang Garden is the oldest famous garden in Suzhou. Built by Su Zimei, a poet in the Song Dynasty, the garden is centered on man-made hills on which there are ancient trees. The famous Canglang Pavilion is hidden among the trees.

The Lion Garden

The Lion Garden is the representative of the gardens of the Yuan Dynasty (1206 – 1368 AD). It is famous for artificial hills piled by rocks from the Taihu Lake. Many of the rocks look like lions in various gestures, hence its name.

The Humble Administrator's Garden

The Humble Administrator's Garden, built in the Ming Dynasty, is divided into three parts: the eastern, middle and western gardens.

The Middle Garden is the essential part. With the pool in the center, the architect designed pavilions, terraces and buildings near the water, and some of them are in the water, with characteristic of areas south of the Yangtze River.

The Liu Garden

The Liu Garden has the style of the gardens of the Qing Dynasty. It takes the pool as the center, while the Hill House of Containing Green and the Building of Bright Zither to the south of the pool are the main buildings; to the north of the pool are artificial hills and pavilions amid trees; to the west, the Veranda of Smelling Sweet-scented Osmanthus on a man-made hill is the best spot to overlook the whole garden and is connected with other places by promenades; the eastern side of the pool is characterized by winding courtyards and corridors. There are three rocky hills. The one in the middle is called Cloud-Capped Hill. It is about nine meters long and is the biggest rock from the Taihu Lake.

杭州 Hangzhou

杭州是浙江省的省会，也是中国七大古都之一。杭州风景秀丽，与苏州共享"上有天堂，下有苏杭"的美誉。

Hangzhou is the capital city of Zhejiang Province and also one of the seven ancient cities in China. With beautiful scenery, it shares with Suzhou the reputation of "up in the sky there is Heaven, down on the earth there are Suzhou and Hangzhou".

坐落在西湖边的杭州市
Hangzhou City is located by the West Lake.

小知识 Knowledge

杭州气候温和，四季分明，物产丰富，特别是这里的丝绸非常著名，深受中外游人的喜爱。

The weather in Hangzhou is mild and there is clear distinction between the four seasons. Hangzhou is rich in products; especially the locally produced silk treasured by visitors.

杭州市交通便利，四通八达，为经济和旅游业发展提供了很好的条件。

杭州是中国著名的旅游城市。主要景点有西湖、岳王庙、虎跑寺、灵隐寺等。

1

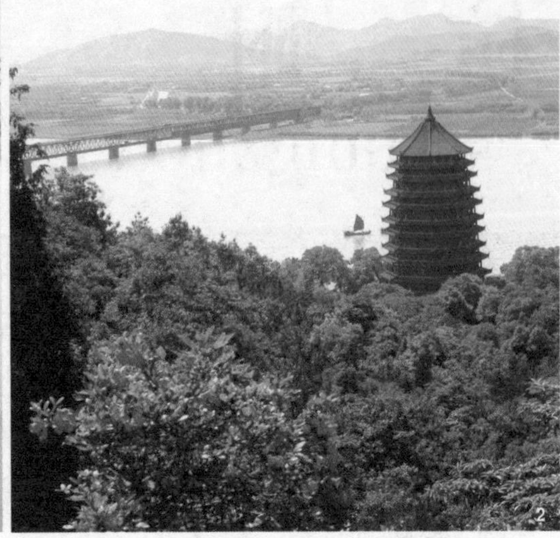
2

西湖

西湖是杭州最著名的景区，三面环山，山水秀丽，景色迷人，文物古迹非常多。

湖中有三座石塔，塔身为球形，中间是空心，夜晚塔中点上蜡烛，烛光倒映在湖面上像一个个小月亮，因此人们称之为"三潭印月"。

六和塔

六和塔建于公元970年，现在塔高59.89米，外檐13层，里面7层，屹立在钱塘江边。

钱塘江大潮

钱塘江大潮是世界上最大的江海潮。它位于杭州市东北方的海盐县境内，每年农历八月十五至八月十八，钱塘江形成特大潮水，非常壮观。

Hangzhou has a convenient transportation network that has laid a good foundation for growth of its economy and tourism.

Hangzhou is a famous tourist city in China, its attractions including the West Lake, Temple of General Yue Fei, Tiger-Running Monastery and the Temple of Inspired Seclusion, etc.

小故事 Anecdote

西湖的湖心亭上有一块石碑，上面写着"虫二"二字。

当年乾隆皇帝来这里游玩，湖心寺方丈请他题匾，他便写了"虫二"二字，众人莫名其妙，一个划船的老人却猜破谜底。原来"虫二"是繁体字"風月"两字的中心笔画，意思是"风月无边"，老人答"水天一色"正好配成对联。

There is a stone tablet in the Mid-lake Pavilion of the West Lake. On the tablet are written two Chinese characters "虫二".

When Emperor Qianlong (1736 – 1796 AD) was on a visit to the West Lake, the abbot of the Mid-lake Monastery requested calligraphy from him. Then the emperor wrote down "虫二", which confused everybody. An elderly boatman nearby figured out the "虫二" are the middle strokes of the complicated form of the two characters "風月(wind and moon, referring to scenery)", meaning "the wonders of natural beauty are boundless", and the old man answered "the water merges with the horizon far beyond", which made a couplet.

West Lake

The West Lake is the most famous tourist spot in Hangzhou. Graceful mountains surround it on three sides. It has charming scenery and many cultural relics and historic sites.

There are three stone pagodas in the middle of the lake. The main body of the pagoda is round and hollow inside. At night, candles are lit in the pagodas, and their reflections on the lake look like many small moons, earning the name "Three Reflections of the Moon in the Water".

The Six-Harmony Pagoda

Built in 970, the Six-Harmony Pagoda, 59.89 m tall, has 13 floors of eaves and seven floors inside. It stands by the Qiangtang River.

Bore of the Qiantang River

The bore of the Qiantang River is the biggest river bore in the world. It exists in Haiyan County to the northeast of Hangzhou City. From August 15-18 in the Lunar Calendar every year, the great tide occurs.

3

小资料 Data

岳王庙里供奉的是南宋民族英雄岳飞。他率领岳家军屡次打败敌人，但是奸臣秦桧却将他害死。后人为了纪念他，便修建了岳王庙。跪在岳王墓前的四个铁人像就是秦桧等几个奸臣。

The Temple of General Yue Fei is dedicated to Yue Fei (1103 – 1142 AD), a national hero of the Southern Song Dynasty (1127 – 1279 AD). He led the Song troops and defeated the enemies many times, until he was betrayed by a treacherous official named Qin Hui (1090 – 1155 AD, Prime Minister of the Southern Song Dynasty detested as a traitor in Chinese history). People of a later generation built the temple to commemorate Yue Fei. The four iron statues kneeling before the tomb of General Yue are the four treacherous officials led by Qin Hui.

1. 西湖
   West Lake
2. 六和塔
   Six-Harmony Pagoda
3. 钱塘潮
   The bore of the Qiantang River

哈尔滨
Harbin

1

哈尔滨位于东北平原北部，是黑龙江省省会。它是中国东北地区重要的工业城市和铁路交通枢纽，也是东北北部航空运输中心之一。

Harbin, located in the north of the Northeast Plain, is the capital city of Heilongjiang Province. It is an important industrial city and the hub of rail transportation in Northeast China and also a regional air transport hub.

小知识 Knowledge

哈尔滨是满语"晒网场"的意思。这个地方原来是一个小渔村，后来修建了铁路，逐渐发展成为一座美丽的城市。

Harbin means "a place for drying nets" in the Manchu language. This place was originally a small fishing village; later, railways were established and it gradually became a thriving and beautiful city.

哈尔滨纬度位置高，与加拿大首都渥太华相近。夏季气候温和，是旅游避暑胜地；冬季气候严寒，冰天雪地，人称"冰城"。1月5日为"冰雪节"，每年这里都要举行盛大的冰灯游园会，各种冰雕、冰灯等艺术品，令人百看不厌。

太阳岛

太阳岛是松花江江心的一个沙岛，岛上树木繁茂，白沙碧水，空气清新，是旅游和疗养的好地方。

Harbin lies at high latitude, similar to that of Ottawa, the capital of Canada. In summer, the weather is mild and it's a good summer resort and tourist place; in winter the weather is freezing and the whole city is covered by snow. January 5 is the day for the annual "Festival of Ice and Snow" featuring a great garden party of ice lanterns, and a display of various ice sculptures and artworks.

Sun Island

Sun Island is a sand island in the middle of the Songhua River, on which trees thrive and which also offers a white beach and fresh air. It is a very good place for tourism and recuperation.

1. 斯大林公园
   Stalin Park
2. 树挂
   Icicles
3. 冰雕
   Ice sculpture
4. 太阳岛雪雕节
   The Snow Sculpture Festival of Sun Island

大连
Dalian

大连位于辽东半岛南端，三面环海，是观赏和游览山、海、礁、岛等自然景观的好去处。

Situated at the southern end of Liaodong Peninsula and surrounded by the sea on three sides, Dalian is a good place for viewing and visiting mountains, the sea and adjacent islands.

1

小资料 Data

大连素有"田径之乡"和"服装城"、"足球城"的盛誉。

Dalian has a reputation as a "city of athletics", "city of fashion" and "city of soccer".

你知道吗 Do you know

大连交通发达，是哈大铁路的终点。大连海港是个不冻港，是东北地区的海上门户。

Dalian has advanced transportation, and it is the terminus for the Harbin-Dalian Railway. The harbor is an ice-free port and also the gateway to the sea for Northeastern China.

大连城市规划合理，绿化面积大，空气清新，整洁优美。它依山傍海，景色秀丽，是中国著名的海滨旅游城市和避暑胜地，每年都吸引着众多游人。

金石滩

金石滩是大连市具有代表性的旅游景点，长7.5千米，奇礁异石特别多，是拥有海滨浴场和海上石林双绝景观的神奇世界。

1. 大连港
The port of Dalian
2. 大连港湾广场
Dalian Bay Center
3. 金石滩
Jinshi Beach

Dalian has benefited from proper urban planning, with a large area of green plants and fresh air that help make it a clean and beautiful city. It lies against mountains and the sea and has graceful scenery. It is a famous seashore tourist city and summer resort, attracting large numbers of visitors every year.

Jinshi Beach

The Jinshi Beach is a representative scenic spot in Dalian. It is 7.5 km long, with many rare reefs and stones. It is a magical world with two unique sights of a seashore bathhouse and a stone forest at sea.

武 汉
Wuhan

武汉是湖北省省会，由武昌、汉口、汉阳三部分组成，又称"武汉三镇"。

武汉是重要的水陆交通枢纽，经济发达，是华中地区重要的经济中心。

Wuhan, the capital city of Hubei Province, comprises the three cities of Wuchang, Hankou and Hanyang.

It is an important hub of water and land transportation. It has an advanced economy and is an important economic center of central China.

1

2

1. 武昌黄鹤楼
The Yellow Crane Tower of Wuhan
2. 东湖
East Lake

武汉市自然风光优美，名胜古迹很多，旅游资源丰富，著名的有东湖、黄鹤楼、武汉长江大桥等。

黄鹤楼

黄鹤楼是中国"四大名楼"之一，始建于公元223年，后屡毁屡建。清朝时又被烧毁，1985年重建，高51.4米，古朴端庄，气宇轩昂。

Wuhan has charming scenery, many historical sites and scenic spots, and rich tourist resources. There are famous tourist spots like the East Lake, the Yellow Crane Tower and the Wuhan Yangtze River Bridge, etc.

Yellow Crane Tower

The Yellow Crane Tower is one of the four famous towers in China. It was first built in 223 and later destroyed and rebuilt many times. In the Qing Dynasty (1644 – 1911 AD), it was burned down again. The tower we see now was rebuilt in 1985. With a height of 51.4 m, it looks classic, graceful and majestic.

小知识 Knowledge

东湖风景区是武汉最大的风景区。湖水清澈，青山环绕，植物种类繁多。东湖盛产多种淡水鱼，特别是武昌鱼最为名贵，可使你大饱口福。

The East Lake is the largest scenic spot in Wuhan. It has crystal-clear water and is surrounded by green mountains with numerous plants. It is rich in freshwater fish, especially the delicious Wuchang fish.

广　州
Guangzhou

1. 广州市容
Guangzhou City
2. 广州五羊雕像
The Five-goat statue represents Guangzhou.

广州是广东省省会，是重要的历史文化名城和旅游城市。

中国实行改革开放的国策之后，广州凭借毗邻港澳的优势率先崛起，成为中国经济最为发达的城市之一。

Guangzhou, the capital city of Guangdong Province, is an important historical and cultural city and tourist city.

After the adoption of the reform and opening up policy, Guangzhou has become one of the most developed cities in China by taking the advantage of bordering Hong Kong and Macao.

1

广州气候温暖湿润，长夏无冬，雨量充沛，四季树叶常青、鲜花盛开，又称"花城"。

越秀公园

越秀公园是广州最大的公园。园内有镇海楼、五羊雕塑、人工湖和许多亭台楼阁及纪念性建筑物。

镇海楼建于明初，高28米，呈长方形，是广州的著名古迹。

白云山风景区

白云山风景区位于广州市北部，是广州著名的休闲和游览胜地。它由30多座山峰组成，最高峰为摩星岭，海拔为383米。

光孝寺

光孝寺是广东省最古老的建筑之一。寺内有东、西两座千佛铁塔，至今有1,000多年的历史。其中，西塔建于963年，是中国目前已知的最古老的铁塔。

小知识 Knowledge

广州别称"羊城"，简称"穗"。

相传周夷王时，有五位仙人骑着口含谷穗的羊降临广州，祝愿此地"永无荒饥"。仙人隐去，五羊化为石像。

Guangzhou has a nickname of "City of Goats", or "Sui" for short.

It is said that during the reign of Emperor Yi of the Zhou Dynasty (885 – 877 BC), there were five immortals that arrived in Guangzhou riding goats holding ears of wheat in their mouths. The immortals prayed that "there would be no starvation" in the place. They then disappeared, and the five goats became stone statues.

2

1. 白云山
The White Cloud Mountains
2. 光孝寺
The Temple of Honor and Filial Piety
3. 广州中山纪念堂
Sun Yat-sen Memorial Hall

Guangzhou has warm and humid climate and a long summer without winter. It has plentiful rain and evergreen trees and blossoming flowers.

Yuexiu Park

Yuexiu Park is the biggest park in Guangzhou, and it includes the Tower Guarding the Sea, the Five-Goat Sculpture, the man-made lake and many pavilions, towers and verandas and memorial buildings.

The Tower Guarding the Sea was built in the early Ming Dynasty (1368 – 1644 AD). It is 28 m tall and in rectangular shape.

The Scenic Spot of White Cloud Mountains

The scenic spot of White Cloud Mountains, located in Northern Guangzhou, is a famous resort for vacationing and tourism. It is made up of more than 30 mountains, among which the highest one is Moxing Peak (383 m).

The Temple of Honor and Filial Piety

The Temple of Honor and Filial Piety is one of the oldest buildings in Guangdong Province. In it there are eastern and western iron towers of one thousand Buddhas, which have a history of over 1,000 years. The western tower was built in 963 and is the oldest iron tower in China.

深 圳
Shenzhen

深圳是中国设立最早的经济特区之一。改革开放以来，发展迅速，现已成为经济发达的现代化都市。

Shenzhen is one of the earliest special economic zones (SEZs) in China. After the reform and opening up, it developed fast and has become a modern city with an advanced economy.

深圳市貌
Shenzhen City

1

2

3

中国民俗文化村

中国民俗文化村占地约20万平方米，是中国第一个集各民族民间艺术、民俗风情和民居建筑于一园的大型文化旅游景区。内含21个民族的24个村寨，有“中国民俗博物馆”之美誉。游客在村寨里可以欣赏和参与各民族的歌舞表演，也可参与制作工艺品和民族风味食品。

西丽湖度假村

西丽湖度假村四面环山，环境幽雅，建筑别致，有典雅的石雕牌楼大门，有1,500多幅精美图案的长廊及高级别墅和游乐场，是一个大众化的游乐园。

锦绣中华微缩景区

锦绣中华微缩景区面积约3平方千米，是世界上面积最大、内容最丰富的微缩景区，拥有万里长城、秦始皇兵马俑坑、北京故宫、杭州西湖、长江三峡、苏州园林等微缩景观。锦绣中华微缩景区是中国历史、文化、艺术、古建筑和民俗风貌的缩影。

世界之窗

世界之窗是深圳又一个大型旅游景区，占地面积为48万平方米。这里有世界上许多著名景观的微缩，如埃及的金字塔、意大利的比萨斜塔、北美的尼亚加拉大瀑布等。

The Village of Chinese Folk Customs and Culture

The Village of Chinese Folk Customs and Culture, covering an area of 200,000 m^2, is the first large-scale cultural tourist spot blending folk arts, folk customs and residential buildings of all ethnic minorities into one park in China. It contains 21 villages of 24 ethnic groups. Tourists can enjoy and even participate not only in the singing and dancing of every ethnic group in the villages but also produce artworks and cook foods.

The Xili Lake Holiday Resort

The Xili Lake Holiday Resort is encircled by mountains. It has elegant surroundings and delicate buildings. There is a classical and elegant stone-carved archway, a promenade with over 1,500 fine paintings, as well as exclusive villas and an amusement park. It is a popular amusement garden.

The Micro-Scenic Spot of Charming and Beautiful China

The Micro-Scenic Spot of Charming and Beautiful China, covering an area of three square kilometers, includes the Great Wall, the Terracotta Warriors and Horses of Emperor Qinshihuang, the Palace Museum of Beijing, the West Lake of Hangzhou, Three Gorges of the Yangtze River, the Gardens of Suzhou and so on, which is the largest micro-scenic facility with the most attractions in the world. It is an epitome of Chinese history, culture, art, classical architecture and folk customs.

Window of the World

Window of the World is another large-scale tourist spot, covering an area of 480,000 m^2. It contains many famous micro-scenic spots in the world, such as the Egyptian Pyramids, Leaning Tower of Pisa of Italy, Niagara Falls of North America, etc.

1. 民俗文化村内的歌舞表演
   The performances at the Village of Chinese Folk Customs and Culture
2. 西丽湖度假村
   The Xili Lake Holiday Resort
3. 锦绣中华景区
   The Micro-Scenic Spot of Charming and Beautiful China
4. 世界之窗
   Window of the World

4

厦门 Xiamen

1

厦门位于福建省境内，是中国东南沿海的重要海港城市。这里气候宜人，冬天不寒冷，夏天也不炎热，是中国著名的旅游、避暑和疗养胜地。

Xiamen, situated in Fujian Province, is an important harbor city along the seacoast of southeast of China. It has pleasant weather——not cold in winter and not too hot in summer. It is a famous summer resort for tourism and recuperation.

2

你知道吗 Do you know

鼓浪屿的海岸线十分曲折，海边有各式各样的礁石和洞穴，海风吹进洞中，发出雷鸣般的涛声，鼓浪屿因此而得名。

Thundering Waves Island has a very winding coastline, along which there are various reefs and caves. When the wind blows into the caves, it produces a thundering sound.

厦门市旅游景点很多，主要有鼓浪屿、南普陀寺、万石岩等。

鼓浪屿

鼓浪屿是厦门的一个小岛，面积不到2平方千米。岛上景色优美，环境幽雅，有“海上花园”的美称。

3

南普陀寺

南普陀寺位于五老山下，有1,000多年的历史，是一座著名的古刹。它位于中国四大佛教名山之一的普陀山之南，所以称南普陀寺。寺内有富丽堂皇的天王殿、大雄宝殿、大悲殿、藏经阁等。

There are many scenic spots in Xiamen, such as the Thundering Waves Island, the South Putuo Temple, the Ten-Thousand-Stone Crag, etc.

Thundering Waves Island

Thundering Waves Island, covering no more than two square kilometers, has beautiful scenery and graceful environment, making it a “garden in the sea”.

South Putuo Temple

South Putuo Temple, located at the foot of Wulao Mountain, has a history of over 1,000 years as an ancient Buddhist temple. Because it lies south of the Putuo Mountain, one of the four famous mountains of Buddhism, it is named the South Putuo Temple. It contains the majestic Hall of Heavenly Kings, the Mahavira Hall, the Hall of Great Mercy and the Tripitaka Pavilion.

小资料 Data

鼓浪屿岛上几乎家家都有钢琴，在这里培育了许多著名的音乐家，所以又有人把鼓浪屿称为“钢琴之岛”。

On the Thundering Waves Island almost every family has a piano, and many famous pianists have been fostered here.

南普陀寺内有一口千年神钟，是宋朝时铸造的。相传当年这口钟被人从土中挖出来，悬挂在梁上时，没人敲它也能发出响声，而且声音能传出好几里远呢！

In the South Putuo Temple, there is a one-thousand-year-old holy bell cast in the Song Dynasty (960 – 1279 AD). It is claimed that the year it was dug out and hung on the beam, it could make sound without being struck and that sound could be heard several kilometers away!

1. 厦门市容
   Xiamen City
2. 鼓浪屿
   Thundering Waves Island
3. 南普陀寺
   South Putuo Temple

昆 明
Kunming

昆明是云南省的省会，是全省政治、经济、文化、科技、交通中心。

Kunming, the capital of Yunnan Province, has beautiful natural scenery. It is the provincial center of politics, economy, culture, technology and transportation.

昆明自然风光优美，气候四季如春，鲜花长开不谢，享有"春城"和"花都"的美誉。但是，昆明昼夜和晴雨之间的温差较大，又有"四季无寒暑，一雨便成冬"的说法。

昆明文物古迹和风景名胜众多，是国际著名风景旅游城市。

大观楼

大观楼坐落在滇池边，高三层，呈方形，红墙绿瓦。登楼远眺，海阔天空，湖光山色，尽收眼底。楼前的一幅180字长联被誉为古今第一长联。

1. 昆明市容
   Kunming City
2. 滇池大观楼
   The Grand View Tower beside Lake Dian
3. 昆明世界园艺博览园
   The Kunming International Horticultural Expo Site

世界园艺博览园场馆

昆明世界园艺博览园场馆，是一组较为宏大的建筑群，占地218公顷，主要有国际馆、中国馆、人与自然馆、大温室、科技馆等建筑。国际馆建筑面积12,006平方米，由一圆形主体和100多米长的弧形墙组成。中国馆占地约20,000平方米，是世博会最大的室内展馆，用于展示绚丽多彩的中国园林园艺。

2

3

The four seasons are all like spring and flowers blossom all year round, so it enjoys the reputation of being a "spring city" and "flower city". However, there is a big difference in temperature between day and night, between sunny days and rainy days. There is a saying which goes "there are no winters and summers, but winter comes after rain".

There are a lot of cultural relics and historical sites and scenic spots in Kunming, which has become a famous international tourist city.

The Grand View Tower

The Grand View Tower, located by Lake Dian, is a three-story square building. It has red walls and green tiles. From the tower one has a panoramic view of boundless sky, beautiful lake and mountains. The long couplet with 180 Chinese characters found here is honored as the longest couplet in ancient and modern times.

The Kunming International Horticultural Expo Site

The Kunming International Horticultural Expo Site is a group of magnificent buildings, covering an area of 218 ha, including the International Stadium, China Stadium, the Stadium of Human and Nature, the Great Greenhouse, the Science Stadium, etc. The International Stadium, with a floor space of 12,006 m^2, is made up of a round main building and an over 100 m–long arc wall. The China Stadium, covering an area of about 20,000 m^2, is the largest interior stadium in the Expo and is used to display the wonders of Chinese gardening.

小资料 Data

1999年5月在昆明举办的世界园艺博览园，使昆明的知名度空前提高，是昆明全方位走向世界的重要里程碑，对昆明乃至云南扩大对外开放，加快经济发展和社会全面进步都有深远的影响。

The Kunming International Horticultural Expo was held in May 1999. It was an important milestone in the opening of the city to the world in an all-round way with far-reaching impact in creating more room for reform and opening up, speeding up economic development and developing a progressive society not only in Kunming but also in the whole of Yunnan Province.

拉　薩
Lhasa

拉萨是西藏自治区首府，是青藏高原上一个历史悠久的"高原古城"。这里全年阳光明媚，所以有"日光城"之称。

Lhasa, the capital of the Tibet Autonomous Region, is an "ancient city on the plateau" with a long history. Here it is sunny all year round, hence a "city of sunshine".

拉萨名胜古迹很多，著名的有布达拉宫、大昭寺等。

1. 布达拉宫
   Potala Palace
2. 十世班禅灵塔
   The 10th Panchan Lama's stupa
3. 大昭寺
   Jokhang Temple

布达拉宫

布达拉宫建筑宏伟，宫墙全部用花岗岩砌筑，是举世闻名的宫堡式建筑群。宫体主楼为13层，高117米，现已被联合国列入世界文化遗产名录。

布达拉宫有5座达赖喇嘛的灵塔，其中十三世达赖的灵塔最高，耗用18,870两黄金包裹，上面镶嵌着各种珠宝。殿内的十三世达赖银像是用1,006两白银铸成的。

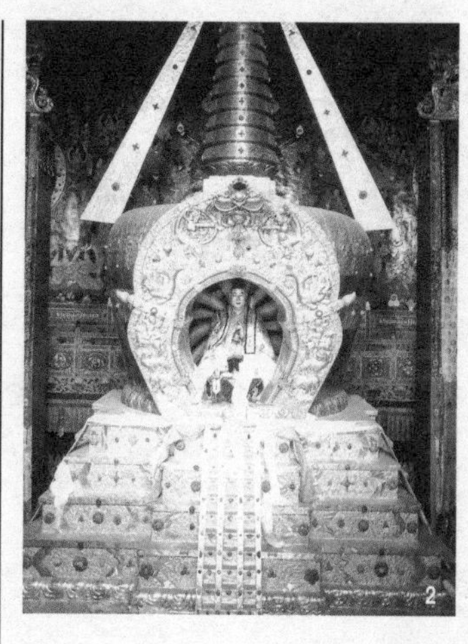

大昭寺

大昭寺位于拉萨市中心，建于公元7世纪，是藏王松赞干布为纪念唐朝文成公主入藏而建的第一座庙宇。

大昭寺以建筑精美、壁画生动而闻名，是西藏的佛教朝拜圣地。

Lhasa has many scenic spots and historical sites, including the famous Potala Palace and Jokhang Temple.

Potala Palace

The magnificent Potala Palace, with its massive granite walls, is a world famous palatial architecture complex. The main building has 13 floors and is about 117 m tall. UNESCO lists it as a World Cultural Heritage.

There are five divine stupas of the Dalai Lamas, among which the stupa for the 13th Dalai Lama is the tallest, being gilded with 943.5 kg of gold and inlaid with various jewels. The 13th Dalai Lama's silver statue was cast using 50.3 kg of silver.

Jokhang Temple

Jokhang Temple, situated in the center of Lhasa, was built in the 7th century and is the first temple built by Songtsan Gambo to commemorate the arrival of Princess Wencheng.

It is famous for its exquisite architecture and vivid mural paintings, and is a holy place for Buddhist pilgrimage in Tibet.

小资料 Data

1951年西藏和平解放，拉萨各方面得到了迅速发展，成为西藏自治区政治、经济、文化中心。

Tibet was liberated peacefully in 1951. Lhasa has developed fast in an all-round way and become the center of politics, economy and culture of the Tibet Autonomous Region.

布达拉宫是唐朝时松赞干布为迎娶文成公主而建的。后来，历代达赖喇嘛不断扩建，形成如今宏大的规模。

The Potala Palace was built by Songtsan Gambo (617 – 650 AD), King of the Tubo Kingdom, when he married Princess Wencheng of the Tang Dynasty. Later, every Dalai Lama expanded it until reaching today's grand size.

西　安
Xi'an

西安是陕西省的省会，是中国东西交通枢纽和西北地区重要的城市。

Xi'an, the capital of Shaanxi Province, is the hub of communications between East and West China and an important city in Northwest China.

1

小资料 Data

西安原名长安，是中国著名的七大古都之一。历史上有11个王朝在这里建都，70多个皇帝在此居住。西安已有3,000多年历史，它与意大利的罗马、希腊的雅典、埃及的开罗合称为"世界四大古城"。

Xi'an was originally named Chang'an, and was one of the seven famous ancient cities in China. Throughout history, there were 11 dynasties that made it their capital, with a total of over 70 emperors living there. Xi'an has a history of over 3,000 years, and it joins Rome, Athens and Cairo as the "four great ancient cities in the world".

西安是中国历史文化名城，名胜古迹非常多，如秦始皇兵马俑博物馆、大雁塔、小雁塔、西安碑林、半坡博物馆、华清池等。

大雁塔

大雁塔初建为5层，唐代武则天当皇帝时，扩建为10层，后被战火破坏。现存7层，塔高64米，是全国重点保护文物。

小雁塔

小雁塔初建时有15层，后来由于多次地震，塔顶两层被震塌，现尚存13层。它造型优美，比大雁塔小，所以叫小雁塔。

明朝时，长安发生地震，小雁塔从顶部往下裂开了一条30多厘米宽的裂缝，后来再次地震，裂缝合拢了。小雁塔共经历了6次地震，3次裂开、3次合拢，塔却不倒，真是神奇。

华清池

华清池是一个古老而著名的温泉，泉水温度为43℃，含有多种化学成分，对人体有医疗保健作用。

半坡遗址

半坡遗址是黄河流域规模最大、保存最完整的原始社会母系氏族村落遗址。

It is a famous historical and cultural city in China. There are many scenic spots and historical sites, such as the Qinshihuang Terracotta Warriors and Horses Museum, Big Wild Goose Pagoda, Xi'an Forest of Steles, Banpo Museum of Neolithic Relics and the Pool of Glorious Purity.

Big Wild Goose Pagoda

When Big Wild Goose Pagoda was first built, it had five storeys. When Wu Zetian (624 – 705 AD, the only empress in Chinese history who ruled China from 690 to 705 AD under the dynastic title of Zhou, which reverted to Tang upon her abdication) ascended to the throne, it was expanded to 10 storeys. Subsequently, it was devastated by wars and fires, and is now only seven storeys, and a height of 64 m. It is one of the key cultural relics under State protection.

你知道吗 Do you know

大雁塔被认为是古西安的象征。它位于慈恩寺内，是唐代高僧玄奘从印度取经回国后倡议建造的，用它来存放经卷。

Big Wild Goose Pagoda is considered to be a symbol of ancient Xi'an. It is situated in the Temple of Benevolence and Kindness. It was built at the suggestion of the eminent monk, Xuanzang (602 – 664 AD), Buddhist scholar, translator and traveler of the Tang Dynasty, whose journey to India is captured in the classic novel *Journey to the West* after he returned from India, to house Buddhist scriptures.

1. 西安市中心的钟楼
   The clock tower in the city center of Xi'an
2. 大雁塔
   Big Wild Goose Pagoda
3. 小雁塔
   Small Wild Goose Pagoda

1. 华清池
Pool of Glorious Purity
2. 半坡遗址
Banpo Ruins

Small Wild Goose Pagoda

Small Wild Goose Pagoda originally had 15 floors, but later, because of frequent earthquakes, the top two floors collapsed leaving the 13 still extant. As it is smaller than the Big Wild Goose Pagoda, although looking most graceful, it was given the name Small Wild Goose Pagoda.

In the Ming Dynasty (1368 – 1644 AD), an earthquake struck Chang'an and a crack over 30 cm wide appeared in the pagoda, only to be closed by another earthquake later. This same thing occurred two more times over the ensuing centuries, but the pagoda remains unscathed, which is a miracle.

你知道吗 Do you know

华清池原来是唐玄宗和杨贵妃沐浴的地方。

The Pool of Glorious Purity was originally the bath place of Emperor Xuanzong (712 – 756 AD) of the Tang Dynasty and his favorite concubine Yang Yuhuan.

Pool of Glorious Purity

The Pool of Glorious Purity is an old famous hot spring whose temperature is about 43ºC. It contains various chemical elements, which has an effect of medical treatment and health care.

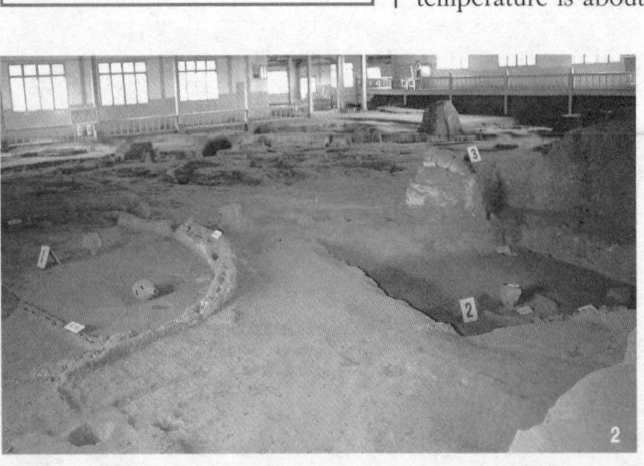

Banpo Ruins

Banpo Ruins is the largest and most complete matrilineal commune of the primitive society in the drainage area of the Yellow River.

呼和浩特
Hohhot

呼和浩特是内蒙古自治区的首府，是一座塞外古城。古城墙用青砖修建，远望是一片青色，所以称之为呼和浩特，即蒙古语"青色的城"的意思。

Hohhot, the capital of the Inner Mongolia Autonomous Region, is an ancient city beyond the Great Wall. The ancient walls are made of gray bricks that give it its name Hohhot, which means "a gray city" in the Mongolian language.

呼和浩特市
Hohhot City

你知道吗 Do you know

"召"是蒙古语"庙"的意思。

"Zhao" means "temple" in the Mongolian language.

呼和浩特寺庙、塔、古迹等文物众多。著名的有大召、小召、席力图召、金刚座舍利宝塔及昭君墓等。

金刚座舍利宝塔

金刚座舍利宝塔又称五塔，是用青砖建成的，塔后照壁上有蒙古文的天文图石刻，是研究古代天文学的重要资料。

大召和席力图召

明朝时，大召是呼和浩特最重要的寺院，到了清乾隆年间，席力图召则成为当地寺院之首，寺内有一座高15米的白石塔，是内蒙古现存最大、最完美的喇嘛塔。

1. 五塔寺
   Wuta Temple
2. 席力图召内的佛像
   The statues of Buddha in the Xilitu Zhao
3. 昭君墓前昭君出塞雕像
   The statue of Wang Zhaojun stands in front of her tomb.

Hohhot has many temples, monasteries, towers and historical sites. They include Big Zhao, Small Zhao, Xilitu Zhao, the Vajra Sarira Stupa and Zhaojun Tomb.

Vajra Sarira Stupa

Vajra Sarira Stupa is built of gray bricks. On the screen wall behind the Stupa there is a stone carving of an astronomical map in Mogolian language, which is important information for researching ancient astronomy.

Big Zhao and Xilitu Zhao

In the Ming Dynasty, Big Zhao was the most important monastery in Hohhot until the reign of Emperor Qianlong of the Qing Dynasty (1736 – 1796 AD), when the Xilitu Zhao became the leading monastery. Of interest is a 15–m–tall white stone dagoba, which is the largest and most complete among existing Lama dagobas.

小资料 Data

王昭君是汉朝美女。当时，匈奴首领向汉元帝求亲，为了结束战争，使人民安宁，王昭君毅然抛弃舒适的宫廷生活，远嫁到这片大草原上。

Wang Zhaojun was a great beauty in the Han Dynasty (206 BC – 220 AD). At that time, the leader of Xiongnu (ancient nomadic people living in the north of China) sought a marriage alliance with Emperor Yuandi (75 – 33 BC) of the Han Dynasty. In order to end war and ensure people could live peacefully, Wang Zhaojun gave up the comfortable royal life resolutely and married the king of Xiongnu on this vast grassland.

2

3

香　港
Hong Kong

香港是中国的特别行政区。面积1,096平方千米，人口678万(2000年11月1日第五次人口普查结果)。

Hong Kong is a special administrative region of China. It has an area of 1,096 km^2 with a population of 6.78 million (according to the fifth census on November 1, 2000).

香港为高度开放的自由港，经济发达，是世界重要的航运、金融和贸易中心之一。这里商品丰富，琳琅满目，有“世界商品橱窗”和“购物天堂”之称。

海洋公园

海洋公园是一座亚洲最大的、具有现代设施和多种娱乐项目的海洋博物馆，由“黄竹坑公园”和“南朗山公园”组成。

天坛大佛

天坛大佛是世界上最大的露天青铜释迦牟尼佛像。大佛高26.4米，重250吨，由200多块青铜板组成。天坛大佛现在已成为香港著名的景观。

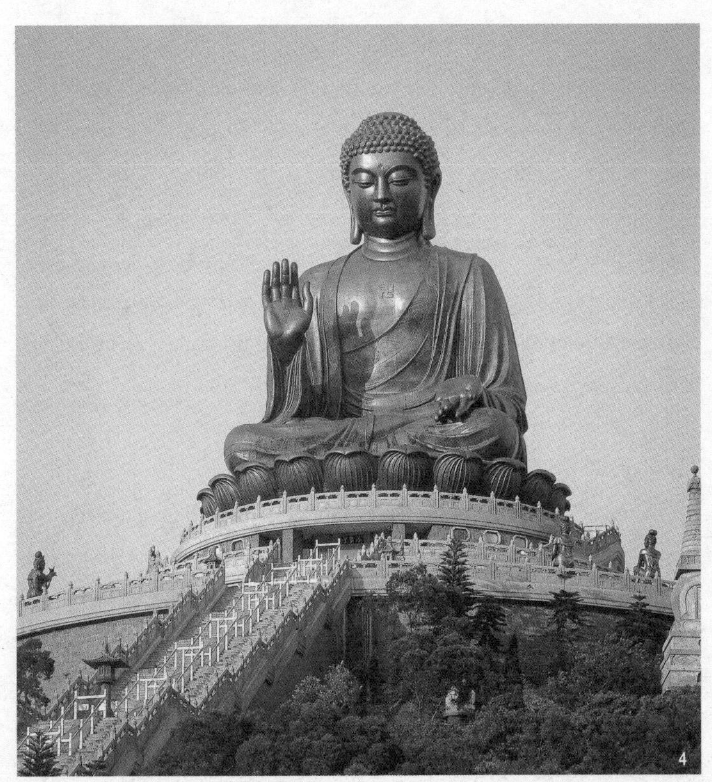

1. 香港维多利亚港景色迷人
   The charming Victoria Habor, Hong Kong
2. 1997年7月1日香港回归政权交接仪式
   The ceremony marking the return of Hong Kong to the motherland on July 1st, 1997
3. 海洋公园海豚表演
   The dolphin show, Ocean Park
4. 宝莲寺天坛大佛
   The Great Buddha of the Temple of Heaven

小资料 Data

1842年8月29日，英国逼迫清朝政府签订了《南京条约》，该条约规定将香港岛割让给英国。1997年7月1日，中国政府恢复对香港行使主权。

On August 29, 1842, Great Britain forced the government of the Qing Dynasty to sign the Treaty of Nanjing ceding Hong Kong Island to Britain. On July 1,1997, the Chinese government resumed sovereignty over Hong Kong.

1. 铜锣湾时代广场
Time Square, Causeway Bay
2. 青马大桥
Tsing Ma Bridge

Hong Kong is a free port with a highly developed economy, and is one of the important centers of shipping, finance and trade in the world. The variety of commodities available is endless, earning it the name of "a show window of the world's commodities" and "shoppers' paradise".

Ocean Park

Ocean Park is the biggest ocean museum in Asia, with modern facilities and various entertainment programs. It is made up of the Huangzhukeng Park and the Nanlang Mountain Park.

The Great Buddha of the Temple of Heaven

The Great Buddha of the Temple of Heaven is the biggest open-air bronze statue of Sakyamuni in the world. With a height of 26.4 m, a weight of 250 tn, it is made up of over 200 blocks of bronze. Now, it has become a famous scenic spot in Hong Kong.

你知道吗 Do you know

在过去，香港是转运广东出产的香料的港口，当地人也以种香料为业，所以被称为香港。

In the past, Hong Kong was a port to transport perfume produced in Guangdong. The local people were also engaged in producing perfume; therefore, it is called Hong Kong (port of perfume).

澳门 Macao

澳门特别行政区位于珠江口的西南岸，由澳门半岛、氹仔岛、路环岛组成，总面积23.5平方千米，人口44万（2000年11月1日第五次人口普查结果）。

The Macao Special Administrative Region, located on the southwest bank of the estuary of the Pearl River, comprises the Macao Peninsular, Dangzai Island and Luhuan Island, covering an area of 23.5 km² with a population of 440,000 (according to the fifth census, November 1, 2000).

小知识 Knowledge

圣保罗教堂牌坊已成为澳门的象征。

The memorial arch of the Church of Saint Paul has become the symbol of Macao.

圣保罗教堂牌坊又称"大三巴"

The memorial arch of the Church of Saint Paul, "*Da San Ba*"

1. 议事亭前地
Largo do Senado
2. 旅游观光塔
Macao Tower
3. 妈阁庙
A-Ma Temple

1

小资料 Data

澳门自古以来就是中国的领土。1553年，葡萄牙殖民者借口要曝晒海水浸湿的货物，强行租用此地。鸦片战争后，澳门被葡萄牙长期占领。1999年12月20日，中国政府恢复对澳门行使主权。

Since ancient times, Macao has been part of China's territory. In 1553, Portuguese colonists made an excuse of drying goods soaked by seawater to make a landing and secure their influence. After the Opium War, Macao was occupied by Portugal. On December 20, 1999, the Chinese government regained sovereignty.

对外贸易、旅游博彩业、建筑地产业和金融业是澳门四大经济支柱。

澳门面积虽小，但人文旅游资源较多，特别以妈阁庙、“大三巴”最为著名。

Foreign trade, tourism and gambling, construction and real estate and financial industries are the pillars of Macao's economy.

Though Macao has a small area, it has rich tourist resources of culture, especially the famous A-Ma (legendary goddess of the sea mainly worshipped in the coastal areas in southeast China) Temple and "*Da San Ba*" (the memorial arch of the Church of Saint Paul).

你知道吗 Do you know

妈阁庙内供奉的是海上保护女神——妈祖（福建语“母亲”的意思），也称天后。每年农历除夕和三月廿三日，渔民都来这里祝寿，香火旺盛。

The A-Ma Temple enshrines the goddess of the sea—A-Ma (it means "mother" in Fujian dialect), also called Empress of the Heaven. Every New Year's Eve and March 23 of the Lunar Calendar, fishermen come to celebrate A-Ma's birthday. It attracts a great number of worshippers and pilgrims.

2

3

旅游胜地
Tourist Attractions

黄　山
Mount Huangshan

黄山位于安徽省南部，是中国著名的风景区，被誉为国之瑰宝、世界奇观，1990年被联合国列入世界自然和文化遗产名录。

Mount Huangshan, situated in the south of Anhui Province, form a famous scenic spot in China honored as a national treasure and a wonder in the world. In 1990, UNESCO listed it as a world natural and cultural heritage site.

1

2

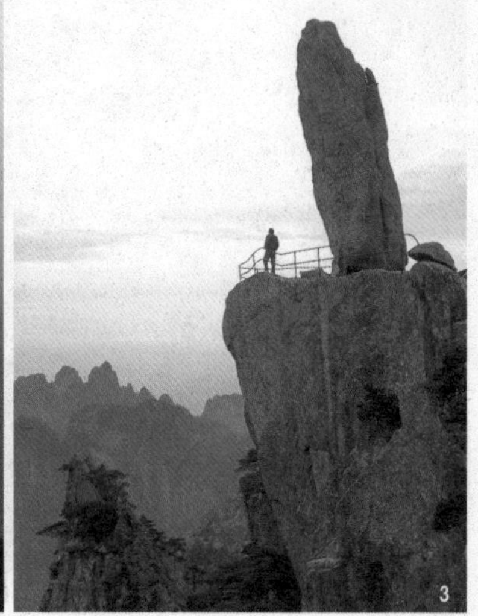

3

黄山素有"中国第一奇山"之誉，险峻、雄伟、奇特、壮观。千米以上的高峰有77座，著名的山峰有30座。最高峰是莲花峰，海拔高度为1,873米；其次为天都峰和光明顶，高度都超过了1,800米。

黄山以"奇松、怪石、云海、温泉"四绝闻名于世。

怪石

黄山的怪石特别多，如莲花峰的岩石呈莲花瓣形状，从远处看它像一朵初开的莲花；飞来石位于飞来峰，底部和山峰截然分开，好像是从天外飞来的一样；在北海散花坞左侧，有一块孤立石峰，顶巅长了棵奇松像花一样，故名"梦笔生花"。

还有如"松鼠跳天都"、"猴子观海"、"天女散花"、"关公挡曹"、"仙人下棋"等，个个都形象逼真，使游客流连忘返。

奇松

黄山的松树大多生长在悬崖峭壁上，扎根在悬岩裂缝中，千姿百态，奇妙绝伦，非常惹人喜爱。

黄山最著名的松树是"迎客松"。它破石而生，挺立在玉屏峰东侧、文殊洞之上，已生长了800多年。它树枝前伸，就像人伸开手臂迎接远方的客人。

1. 黄山号称"中国第一奇山"
   Mount Huangshan is considered to be "the most peculiar mountain in China".
2. 黄山松
   The pine trees of Mount Huangshan
3. 飞来石
   The Rock Which Flew from Afar

小知识 Knowledge

因为黄山山峰的石壁是黑色的，所以在秦朝的时候称它为黟山，意思是黑山。相传轩辕皇帝在此炼丹成仙，后来，信奉道教的唐明皇下令将黟山改称为黄山，意思是黄帝之山。

Because the cliffs of Mount Huangshan are black, they were originally called the Yi (Yi meaning black) Mountains in the Qin Dynasty over 2,000 years ago. It is said that the Yellow Emperor Xuanyuan (legendary ancestor of the Chinese nation) made pills of immortality here and became an immortal. Later, Emperor Minghuang (712 – 756 AD) of the Tang Dynasty, who believed in Taoism, issued an order changing the Yi Mountains into Mount Huangshan, meaning the mountains of the Yellow Emperor.

云海

黄山四季都有壮观的云海，每当云海出现时，山峰时隐时现，特别是夕阳斜照而有云雾时，有时会出现一种彩色的光环。人在光环之中，人动影亦动，这就是著名的"宝光"，也叫"佛光"。

1. 壮观的云海
   The splendid cloud sea
2. 仙境般的黄山
   Magnificent Mount Huangshan
3. 冬日黄山松
   The pine trees of Mount Huangshan in winter
4. 温泉是黄山"四绝"之一
   The hot spring is one of the four unique scenes in Mount Huangshan.

温泉

朱砂温泉是黄山最著名的温泉。每隔若干年，水色就会变红，经过六七天后方逐渐变清。其水温一般在42℃，水质清澈，可以饮用，可以沐浴，具有医疗价值。

Mount Huangshan, precipitous and magnificent, is usually considered as "the most peculiar mountain in China". There are 77 peaks over 1,000 m high, among which 30 peaks are famous. The highest one is the Lotus Peak (1,873 m), followed by the Peak of Celestial City and the Peak of Brightness, both above 1,800 m.

Mount Huangshan is famous for four unique scenes—peculiar pine trees, strange rocks, cloud seas and hot springs.

Strange Rocks

There are numerous strange rocks on Mount Huangshan. For example, rocks on the Lotus Peak look like a lotus in blossom when seen from afar; the Rock Which Flew from Afar on the Peak Which Flew from Afar is separated from the peak as if it flung from far away; at the left side of the Valley of the North Sea Disseminating Flowers, there is an isolated rock peak on top of which grows a peculiar pine tree like a flower, namely the "Blooming in Dream".

 **小资料 Data**

黄山风景区方圆154平方千米，号称"五百里黄山"。

The Mount Huangshan Scenic Spot has an area of about 154 km^2. It is also called "500 *li* (250 km) Mount Huangshan".

In addition, there are rocks like "Squirrel Jumps over the Celestial City", "Monkey Views the Sea", "Celestial Girls Scattering Flowers", "Lord Guan Blocks the Way of Cao Cao", "Immortals Play Chess" and so on, each of which looks vivid and makes tourists reluctant to leave.

2

Strange Pine Trees

Pine trees of Mount Huangshan mainly grow on the cliffs or are rooted in the cracks between rocks. They are all different in posture.

The most famous pine tree on Mount Huangshan is the so-called "Guests-Greeting Pine Tree" which comes out of rocks and stands upright over the Cave of Wisdom east of the Peak of the Jade Screen. It is more than 800 years old. Its front branches stretch forward as if it is spreading its arms to greet guests from far away.

3

Cloud Sea

There is splendid cloud sea on Mount Huangshan. When the cloud sea appears, peaks emerge and disappear from time to time. Especially at sunset, there sometimes appears a colorful aureole that encircles people. When you move, the aureole also moves. This is the famous "treasure light", also "Buddha's halo".

Hot Springs

The Vermillion Hot Spring is the most famous hot spring on Mount Huangshan. Every a few years, the water becomes red, before gradually clearing after six or seven days. Its temperature usually stays at 42°C. The water is very clear, and drinking it also has medicinal value.

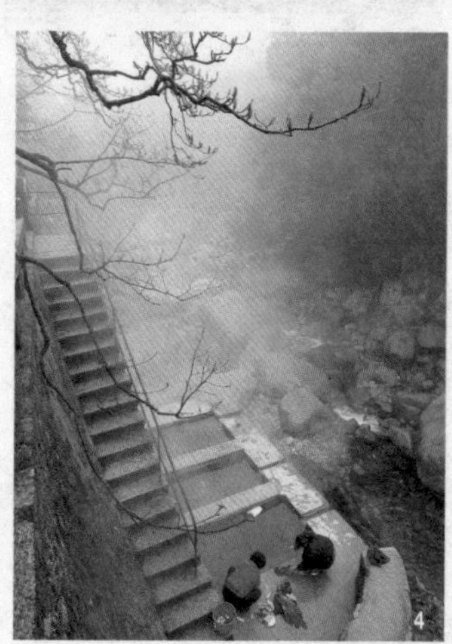
4

庐　山
Mount Lushan

庐山位于江西省北部，以“雄、奇、险、秀”闻名于世，风景优美，气势雄伟，夏季凉爽宜人，是闻名中外的旅游和避暑胜地，现已被联合国列入世界文化遗产名录。

Mount Lushan, situated in the north of Jiangxi Province, is famous for "grandeur, peculiarity, danger and elegance". It has beautiful scenery and a cool summer, making it a world famous summer resort and a world cultural heritage site listed by UNESCO.

1. 庐山
   Mount Lushan
2. 含鄱口
   The Hanpo Entrance
3. 三叠泉
   The Three-Fold Spring

庐山共有99座山峰，每座山峰都巍峨挺拔，雄伟壮观。主峰大汉阳峰海拔1,474米。

庐山景点非常多，著名的有三叠泉、龙首崖、三宝树、五老峰、仙人洞、含鄱口等。

三叠泉

三叠泉是“庐山第一奇观”，高100多米，依着山体分为上、中、下三级，所以又叫“三级泉”。它从高高的山上凌空下泻，就像水帘悬挂在空中，因此又称它为“水帘泉”。

含鄱口

含鄱口位于含鄱岭上，面对鄱阳湖，是看日出的好地方。

三宝树

三宝树是三棵高耸如云的古树，相传是晋朝人种植的。一棵是银杏树，另外两棵是柳杉树。每棵宝树都高达40多米，枝叶繁茂。

小资料 Data

相传在周朝时，有匡氏七兄弟结伴到庐山修行，因此庐山也称匡庐。

It is said that in the Zhou Dynasty (1100 – 256 BC) there were seven brothers of the Kuang Family who came to cultivate their way, so Mount Lushan is also called the Kuang Mountain.

2

3

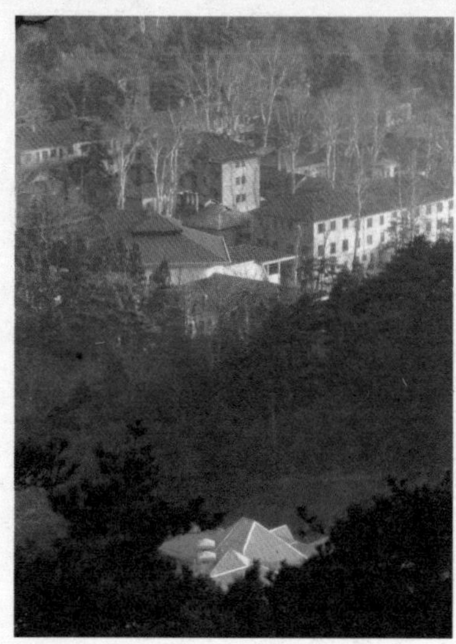

庐山别墅
The villas on the Mount Lushan

There are altogether 99 peaks and each is towering and splendid. The main peak, the Great Hanyang Peak, stands 1,474 m above the sea level.

There are many attractions on Mount Lushan, such as the famous Three-Fold Spring, Cliff of the Dragon's Head, Three-Treasure Trees, Five-Elder Peak, Immortal Cave, Hanpo Entrance, etc.

The Three-Fold Spring

The Three-Fold Spring is "the first wonder of Mount Lushan". Over 100 m tall, it is divided into three levels along the mountain—upper, middle and lower levels, so it is also called "Three-Level Spring". It pours down from the high mountain like a water curtain hanging in the air, so it has another name "Spring of Water Curtain".

The Hanpo Entrance

The Hanpo Entrance, located on Hanpo Peak facing Poyang Lake, is a good place to view the sunrise.

The Three-Treasure Trees

The Three-Treasure Trees are three ancient trees towering into the sky, and said to have been planted by people in the Jin Dynasty (265 - 420 AD). One is ginkgo and the other two are cryptomeria. Each of them reaches 40 m or so and is a mass of branches and leaves.

你知道吗 Do you know

庐山是著名的避暑胜地。在烈日炎炎的七月，平均气温只有22℃，早晚更加凉爽。山中别墅很多，具有英、美、法、俄、德等多个国家建筑风格的就有940幢，它们大多用石头或木头建成。

Mount Lushan is a famous summer resort. In sweltering July, its average temperature is only 22°C and even cooler in the morning and at night. There are many villas on the mountains, among which 940 are of the architectural styles of Britain, America, France, Russia and Germany, as the area was popular with foreign residents of China in the first part of the 20th century. They are mostly built of stone or wood.

武夷山
Mount Wuyi

武夷山位于福建省西北部。这里碧水丹山，奇险秀丽，自古就以“奇秀甲东南”著称于世，现已被联合国列入世界自然和文化遗产名录，被称为“世界生物之窗”。

Mount Wuyi, situated in the northwest of Fujian Province, has green water and peaks that are fantastic, precipitous, elegant and beautiful. Since ancient times, it has enjoyed the reputation of being "the most marvelous and elegant mountain in the southeast". UNESCO lists it as a world natural and cultural heritage. It is known as a "biological showcase of the world".

武夷山一景
Landscape of Mount Wuyi

武夷山共有36座山峰，造型奇特，千姿百态，引人入胜。主要有三仰峰、大王峰、玉女峰、天游峰等。其中三仰峰高度为717.7米，是武夷山最高峰。

九曲溪

武夷山的精华在九曲溪。九曲溪就是溪水共弯九曲，全长约7.5千米，溪水碧清，曲曲弯弯，武夷山著名的山峰都列在溪边。乘竹筏游九曲溪，可以看两岸的美景，这是游武夷山最精彩的节目。

玉女峰

玉女峰是武夷山最迷人、最秀丽的山峰，就像仙女下凡一样，屹立在九曲溪边。

大王峰

大王峰端庄雄伟，具有王者风范，所以人们都叫它“大王峰”。山峰顶大腰细，仿佛是顶纱帽，又称它为纱帽岩。大王峰四壁陡峭，只能从一条裂缝中的爬梯登上山顶。

天游峰

天游峰为“武夷第一胜地”。这里云雾多，是看云海的最佳地方，在峰顶可以看到九曲溪全景。

1. 九曲溪
The Nine-Curve Stream
2. 玉女峰
Jade Lady Peak
3. 大王峰
Great King Peak

Mount Wuyi contains 36 peaks that adopt different postures. The main ones are the Three-Admiration Peak, Great King Peak, Jade Lady Peak, Peak of Heavenly Tour and so on. Among them, the Three-Admiration Peak is 717.7 m high, the highest peak of Mount Wuyi.

The Nine-Curve Stream

The essence of Mount Wuyi is the Nine-Curve Stream, which has nice curves and is about 7.5 km long. The stream is green and crystal clear and winds its way among the mountains. If you take a bamboo raft to visit the Nine-Curve Stream, you can enjoy the beautiful scenery on both banks.

你知道吗 Do you know

武夷山既是千年文化名山，又是道教的发源地之一。

Mount Wuyi is one of the original places of Taoism.

Jade Lady Peak

Jade Lady Peak, the most charming and elegant peak of Mount Wuyi, looks like a fairy descending to the world. It is located by the Nine-Curve Stream.

3

Great King Peak

Great King Peak, grand and solemn, has the demeanor of a king, hence its name. The peak's top is thicker than its middle part, giving the appearance of a gauze hat (a hat worn by an official in olden times), so it's also called the Gauze Hat Rock. It has precipitous cliffs, and there is only one way to the top.

Peak of Heavenly Tour

The Peak of Heavenly Tour is the best place to view the cloud sea. From the top you can also have a panoramic view of the Nine-Curve Stream.

武陵源
Wulingyuan

1. 云雾缭绕的天子山
   Tianzi Mountain surrounded by cloud
2. 张家界
   Zhangjiajie
3. 金鞭溪
   Golden Whip Stream

武陵源风景区位于湖南省西北部，包括张家界国家级森林公园、索溪峪自然保护区和天子山自然保护区三部分。拥有原始森林景观，素有“峰三千，水八百”之称，现已被联合国列入世界自然遗产名录。

Wulingyuan Scenic Spot, situated in the northwest of Hunan Province, includes Zhangjiajie National Forest Park, Suoxiyu Nature Reserve and Tianzi Mountain Nature Reserve. It has virgin forests and boasts of "3,000 peaks and 800 streams and lakes". UNESCO lists it as one of the world natural heritage sites.

张家界

张家界是中国第一个国家级森林公园。这里森林资源极其丰富，植物种类繁多。景点有60多处，主要有金鞭石、六奇阁、清风亭等。

索溪峪风景区

索溪峪风景区是武陵源风景区的中心和门户，风景独特，主要有22个景点，以天台和西海最为著名。

天台四周是悬崖峭壁，游客要登上天台，唯一的道路是72级用钢管焊接而成的"天梯"。

天子山风景区

天子山风景区主要有仙女桥、一步难行等景观。其山峰具有高、多、奇的特点。

一步难行景观是两块高耸入云的巨石，在中间裂开一条缝，缝隙宽度不到1米。经过这里时，如果看下面的万丈深渊，你就会双脚发软，不敢跨过去，所以称它为"一步难行"。

你知道吗 Do you know

张家界有三大奇观：一是奇怪的光圈，西海上空每年会出现一次美丽的光圈，光圈由小变大，大约持续3~4分钟；二是奇怪的月亮，春、夏季久雨未晴的晚上，天上会出现红月亮；三是奇怪的影子，秋高气爽的好天气，人的身影会一变二，二变三，令人诧异。

There are three wonders in Zhangjiajie. One is strange aureole. Every year, a beautiful aureole appears in the sky over the West Sea, becoming bigger and bigger and lasting for three to four minutes. Second is the strange moon; at night after a long period of rain in spring and summer, a red moon emerges in the sky. Third is the strange shadow; in fine autumn weather, a person's shadow can change from one to two, and from two to three, which is astonishing.

2

3

小知识 Knowledge

金鞭石因其形状像鞭子，岩石呈金黄色而得名。它拔地而起，三面笔陡，金光闪烁，气势雄伟。

The Golden Whip Rock got its name because it is shaped like a whip and its color is golden. It has sheer cliffs and looks majestic.

Zhangjiajie

Zhangjiajie is the first national forest park in China. It has rich forest resources and numerous species of plants. There are over 60 scenic attractions, such as the Golden Whip Rock, the Six-Wonder Pavilion and the Breeze Pavilion.

Suoxiyu Scenic Spot

The Suoxiyu Scenic Spot is the center and gateway of Wulingyuan. There are 22 main attractions, among which the Heavenly Terrace and the West Sea are the most famous.

1. 天子山自然保护区
   Tianzi Mountain Nature Reserve
2. 黄龙洞
   Huanglong Cave

Tianzi Mountain Scenic Spot

The Tianzi Mountain Scenic Spot includes the Celestial Lady Bridge, Hard to Move One Step and so on. There are many peaks here that are high and special.

Hard to Move One Step is a crack less than one meter wide between two huge rocks towering into the sky. If you pass here and look down into the abyss, you will feel frightened and could hardly move, hence its name.

武当山 Mount Wudang

武当山位于湖北省西北部，是著名的道教胜地之一。山峦清秀，风景清幽。大小山峰共有72座，主峰天柱峰海拔1,612米。武当山现已被联合国列入世界文化遗产名录。

Mount Wudang, located in the northwest of Hubei Province, is one of the famous holy places of Taoism as well as one of the world cultural heritage sites listed by UNESCO. The mountains are elegant and the scenery is secluded. There are altogether 72 peaks, among which the main peak is 1,612 m above sea level.

位于天柱峰的太和宫
Taihe Palace sits right by the Tianzhu Peak.

1. 太极剑
Taichi fencing
2. 金殿
The Golden Palace

小知识 Knowledge

武当山不仅以道教著称，而且还以拳术、剑术闻名于世。

Mount Wudang is famous not only for Taoism but also for boxing and fencing.

小故事 Anecdote

相传仙人张三丰曾经在遇真宫修炼，他擅长武术，精通医术，被武当山道门视为祖师之一。

It is said that the Immortal Zhang Sanfeng once practiced asceticism in the Palace of Genuine Meeting. He was good at martial arts and proficient in medical skills. He was considered to be one of the founders of the Taoist Sect of Mount Wudang.

武当山的古代建筑非常有名，大多为建于明朝永乐年间的道教宫观，当时有8宫、2观、36庵堂、72岩庙，保存到现在的以金殿最为有名。

金殿

金殿在武当山主峰的峰顶。大殿全部用铜铸鎏金构件组装而成。重檐瓦脊上分立着68个铜兽，个个玲珑精巧，栩栩如生。殿内的宝座上，供着真武大帝披发跣足的铜铸鎏金塑像，重达5,000多千克。

The ancient constructions on Mount Wudang are very famous, being mostly Taoist temples built in the Yongle imperial reign (1403 – 1425 AD) of the Ming Dynasty. At that time, there were eight palaces, two Taoist temples, 36 nunneries and 72 rock temples. Among those still surviving is the Golden Palace.

The Golden Palace

The Golden Palace, on the top of the main peak, is made up of components cast in copper and gilded by gold. On the ridges of the double-eaved roof stand 68 copper beasts, each delicate and vivid. On the throne in the Palace is enshrined a copper, gold-gilded statue of the loose haired and barefooted God of Genuine Power. It weights over 5,000 kg.

泰　山 Mount Tai

泰山日出
Sunrise over Mount Tai

泰山位于山东省中部，是“五岳”中的东岳，为“五岳”之首，现已被联合国列入世界自然和文化遗产名录。

Mount Tai, situated in the middle of Shandong Province, is the easternmost mountain and the leading one of the “five sacred mountains”. Now, UNESCO lists it as one of the world natural and cultural heritage sites.

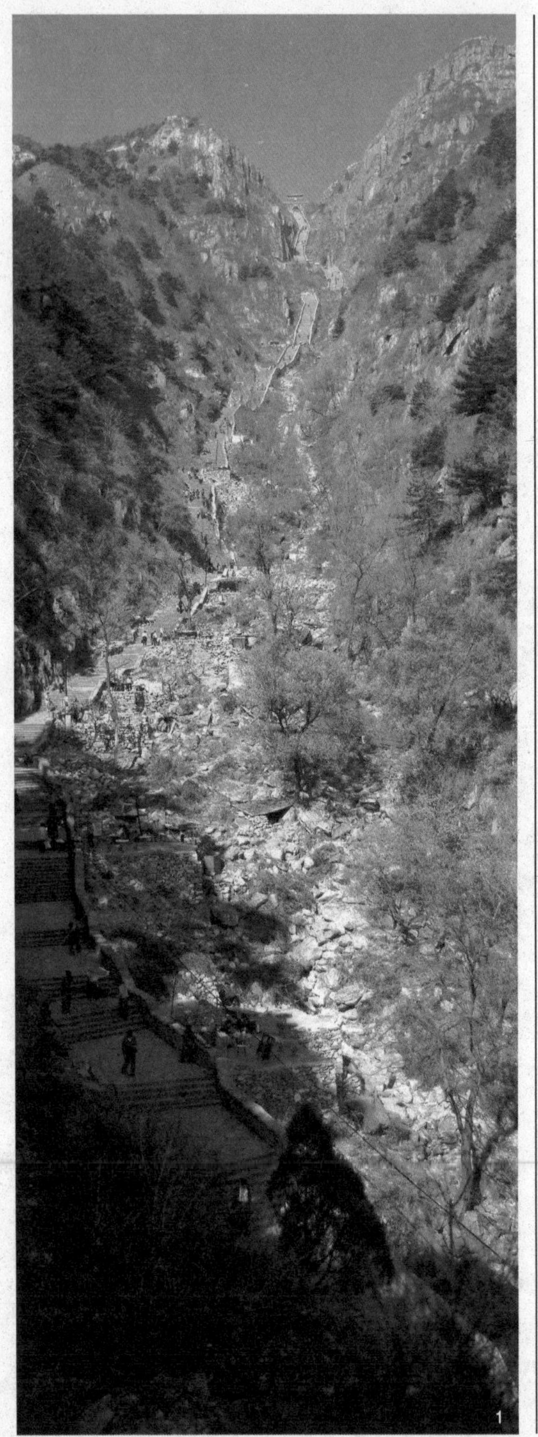

泰山耸立于华北平原东侧，山体高大，巍峨壮观，著名的山峰有玉皇顶等。

玉皇顶

玉皇顶是泰山最高峰，海拔1,538.2米。山顶上有玉皇庙，古时候登山祭天就在这里设祭坛。这里也是看日出和云海的好地方。

南天门

南天门又称"三天门"，是登泰山的最后一道门坊，也是泰山顶的大门。

泰山的日出和云海非常壮观、美丽，特别是在玉皇顶的日观峰上看日出、观云海更是令人赏心悦目。

岱庙

泰山的古代建筑特别多，山下的岱庙是中国历代皇帝拜"泰山神"的地方。

岱庙坊在岱庙的正阳门外，古代帝王来泰山祭祀首先在这里举行简短仪式，然后才到岱庙举行正式大祭。

天贶殿是岱庙的主殿，建于宋代，是古代帝王来泰山祭祀"泰山神"的地方。主殿的殿壁上有幅巨型壁画，长62米，高3.3米，描绘了"泰山神"出巡和归来的场景，是件艺术珍品。

1. 泰山"十八盘"
The "Eighteen Spirals" of Mount Tai
2. 泰山
Mount Tai

Soaring to the east of the North China Plain, Mount Tai is majestic with many famous peaks, the best known being the Peak of Jade Emperor.

The Peak of Jade Emperor

The Peak of Jade Emperor is the highest peak of Mount Tai, with an altitude of 1,538.2 m. On the summit there is the Temple of Jade Emperor. In ancient times, people would scale the mountain and set up sacrificial altars to offer sacrifices to heaven. It is also a good place to view the sunrise and cloud sea.

The South Heaven Gate

The South Heaven Gate, also called the "Three-Heaven Gate", is the last gate on the climb to the summit of Mount Tai.

The sunrise and cloud sea of Mount Tai are very splendid and beautiful, especially when seen from the Peak of Jade Emperor.

你知道吗 Do you know

在登泰山的途中，有个闻名中外的经石峪。在斜坡石壁上，刻着隶书《金刚经》经文，原来有2,500多字，经过1,400多年的风吹雨打，现在还残存着1,043个字。每个字有50厘米见方，被人们誉为"大字鼻祖"。

On the way up Mount Tai, there is a world-famous Valley of Scripture Stone. On the rock cliff is carved the scripture of the *Vajracchedika Sutra* in official script (an ancient style of calligraphy current in the Han Dynasty). There were originally over 2,500 characters, but, after 1,400 years of rain and wind, only 1,043 remain. Every character is about 50 cm long and 50 cm wide, and the whole thing is honored as the "ancestor of large-sized characters".

The Temple to the God of Mount Tai

There are many ancient buildings on Mount Tai. The Temple to the God of Mount Tai at the foot of Mount Tai is the place where Chinese emperors of every dynasty worshipped "God of Mount Tai".

The Memorial Arch of the Temple to the God of Mount Tai is outside of the Zhengyang Gate. In ancient time, emperors would hold a short and simple rite before they held the formal ceremony of offering sacrifices.

The Heavenly Grant Palace, the main palace of the Temple to the God of Mount Tai, was built in the Song Dynasty (960 – 1279 AD) and is a place where ancient emperors offered sacrifices to the "God of Mount Tai". On the wall there is a huge mural 62 m long and 3.3 m high that describes how the God of Mount Tai went on a tour of inspection. It is a rare work of art.

你知道吗 Do you know

北京的故宫、曲阜的孔庙和岱庙被誉为中国三大宫殿建筑群。

The Palace Museum of Beijing, the Confucius Temple of Qufu and the Temple to the God of Mount Tai are reputed to be the three great palace buildings.

1. 岱庙坊
The Memorial Arch of the Temple to the God of Mount Tai
2. 岱顶
Mount Tai Peak

嵩　山
Mount Song

嵩山位于河南省中部，是“五岳”中的中岳，主要由太室山和少室山组成。

Mount Song, situated in the middle of Henan Province, is the middle mountain of "the five sacred mountains", and is comprised of Taishi Mountain and Shaoshi Mountain.

嵩山
Mount Song

嵩山有72座山峰，山峰奇特，山色秀丽。最高峰是太室山，高度为1,440米。山下有72座寺庙，是佛教、道教、儒教三教汇集的地方，庙内文物众多，有“文物之乡”的美称。

中岳庙

中岳庙是古代帝王祭祀山神的地方，大小殿阁楼亭有400多间，是中国著名的古建筑群之一。

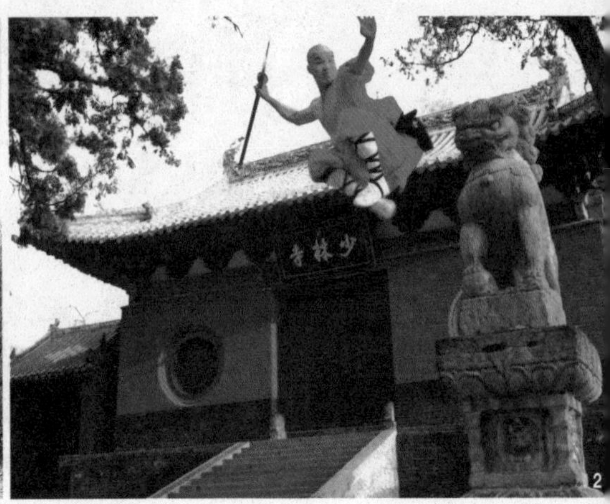

1. 中岳庙
The Zhongyue Temple
2. 少林和尚习武
Shaolin monks practicing martial arts
3. 塔林
The Forest of Stupas
4. 中岳庙内的铁人
The iron statues of the Zhongyue Temple

少林寺

少室山上的少林寺，在唐朝时被称为"天下第一名刹"，是中国佛教禅宗发源地。少林武功更是闻名世界，被奉为"武林之尊"。

千佛殿是少林寺内规模最大的殿堂。殿内的三面墙上有大型的彩色壁画，面积300多平方米，为著名唐代画家吴道子所作。

少林寺的塔林，是历代和尚的墓塔，现在有220多座，是中国现存最大的塔林。塔的大小、形状各不相同，有圆柱形、锥形、瓶形。有的高达7～8米，有的只有1米左右。

Mount Song has 72 peculiar and elegant peaks. The highest peak is Taishi Mountain (1440 m). At the foot of Mount Song there are 72 temples for Buddhism, Taoism and Confucianism with a huge collection of cultural relics, earning the area a reputation as a "land of cultural relics."

The Zhongyue Temple

The Zhongyue Temple was the place where the ancient emperors offered sacrifices to the god of mountains. There are 400 palaces, verandas, towers and pavilions. It is one of the famous ancient buildings in China.

小资料 Data

中岳庙内有四个高大的铁人，铸造于宋朝。每个高4米，重1.5吨，个个双眼圆睁，威严无比。

In the Zhongyue Temple stand four tall iron statues cast in the Song Dynasty. Each is 4 m tall and weighs 1.5 tn. With their eyes wide open, they look solemn and dignified.

The Shaolin Monastery

The Shaolin Monastery on the Shaoshi Mountain was called "the most famous monastery" in the Tang Dynasty, and was the originating place of Zen Buddhism. The martial arts of the Shaolin Monastery are held in highest regard around the world.

The Thousand-Buddha Hall is the largest in the Shaolin Monastery. On three walls are large colorful murals with an area of over 300 m^2 that were painted by Wu Daozi, a famous Tang Dynasty painter.

The Forest of Stupas contains the tombs of monks of every generation, and there are now more than 220. It is the biggest existing forest of stupas in China. They vary in size and shape, some being cylindrical, some cones, while others are like jars; they range in height from one to eight meters.

4

3

你知道吗 Do you know

"五岳"是指中国五大名山，它们分别是东岳泰山、西岳华山、中岳嵩山、南岳衡山、北岳恒山。

"The five sacred mountains" refer to the five most famous mountains in China. They are the eastern Mount Tai, the western Mount Hua, the central Mount Song, the southern Mount Heng and the northern Mount Heng.

峨眉山
Mount Emei

峨眉山位于四川省境内，是中国四大佛教名山之一。峨眉山青峰叠翠，风景秀丽，有“峨眉天下秀”的美誉。峨眉山及附近的乐山大佛，已被联合国列入世界自然和文化遗产。

Mount Emei, situated in Sichuan Province, is one of the four famous mountains of Buddhism in China. Green mountains undulate and trees overlap each other on Mount Emei, giving it a reputation as "the most graceful mountain on Earth". UNESCO lists Mount Emei and the Giant Buddha of Leshan as one of the world natural and cultural heritage sites.

1. 峨眉金顶
The Golden Peak of Mount Emei
2. 峨眉山
Mount Emei

峨眉山是供奉普贤菩萨的佛山。山中寺庙很多，主要有报国寺、伏虎寺、万年寺，其中规模最大、最宏伟的是报国寺。

金顶

峨眉山的金顶海拔为3,077米，在金顶上看"佛光"是游人的愿望，"佛光"使峨眉山富有神秘色彩，游客能看到"佛光"的都感到万分荣幸。

每当天空晴朗，没有风的时候，在下午两三点钟以后，人们站在金顶的舍身崖上，俯身下望，有时会看到五彩光环浮于云际，自己的身影置于光环之中，影随人移，互不相失。无论有多少人并排观看，他们所看到的始终是自己的身影。过去，人们解释不了这种现象，认为是"佛光"。其实，这不过是太阳光、云层和人体三者处在45°斜线上的时候所产生的折射现象。

伏虎寺的传说

宋朝时，该寺叫神龙堂。后来，寺庙附近出现了猛虎，经常伤人，庙里的和尚建立了一尊胜幢，从此以后，老虎没有了，寺名就改为伏虎寺。

Mount Emei is a Buddhist mountain enshrining the Bodhisattva of Universal Benevolence. There are many temples on the mountain, including the Temple of Serving the Country, the Tiger-Taming Temple and the Ten-Thousand-Year Temple. Among them, the biggest and most magnificent one is the Temple of Serving the Country.

小资料 Data

报国寺是在明朝时候修建的。寺内有一尊巨大的瓷佛，高2.4米，是1415年在景德镇烧制的，为稀世珍品。

The Temple of Serving the Country was built in the Ming Dynasty. In it, there is a huge porcelain statue of Buddha 2.4 m tall, which was made in Jingdezhen in 1415. It is considered a national treasure.

你知道吗 Do you know

万年寺的骑象菩萨重62吨，高7.3米。它已经有1,000多年的历史。

The statue of the Bodhisattva on an elephant in the Ten-Thousand-Year Temple weighs 62 tn and has a height of 7.3 m. It has a history of over 1,000 years.

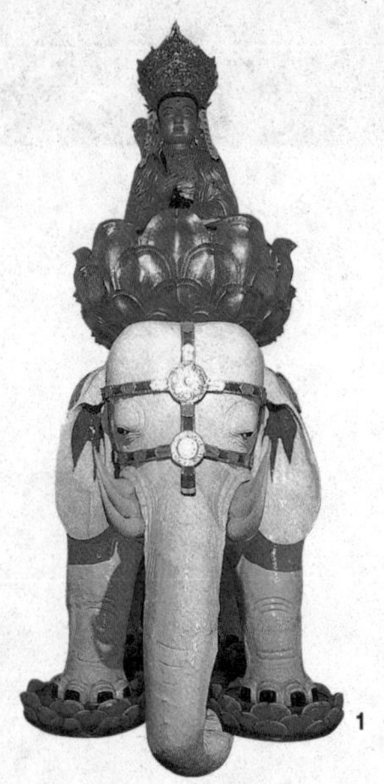

1. 万年寺内的骑象菩萨
   The statue of a Bodhisattva seated on an elephant
2. 万年寺
   Ten-Thousand-Year Temple
3. 峨眉“佛光”
   The “Buddha's halo” of Mount Emei

The Golden Peak

The Golden Peak of Mount Emei is 3,077 m above sea level. To view the “Buddha's halo” is the wish of many tourists.

When it's sunny and there is no wind, after two or three o'clock in the afternoon, if you stand on the Sheshen Cliff of the Golden Peak and look down, sometimes you will see a colorful aureole floating over the clouds. Your body will appear in the aureole, and, when you move, the aureole moves with you. No matter how many people stand together viewing it, they always see their own shadows. In the past, people couldn't explain this phenomenon and thought it was “Buddha's halo”. Actually, it is a phenomenon of refraction.

The Legendary Tiger-Taming Temple

In the Song Dynasty, the Tiger-Taming Temple was called the Hall of Magical Dragon. Later, ferocious tigers appeared near the temple and often attacked people, so the monks built a holy pillar inscribed with the name of the Buddha; after that, the tigers disappeared and so it was renamed the Tiger-Taming Temple.

乐山大佛
The Giant Buddha of Leshan

乐山大佛位于四川省乐山市的凌云山上，在岷江、青衣江、大渡河三江的汇合处，是世界上最大的石刻佛像。

The Giant Buddha of Leshan is located on Lingyun Mountain in Leshan City, Sichuan Province and at the convergence of the Min, Qingyi and Dadu rivers. It is the biggest stone statue of Buddha in the world.

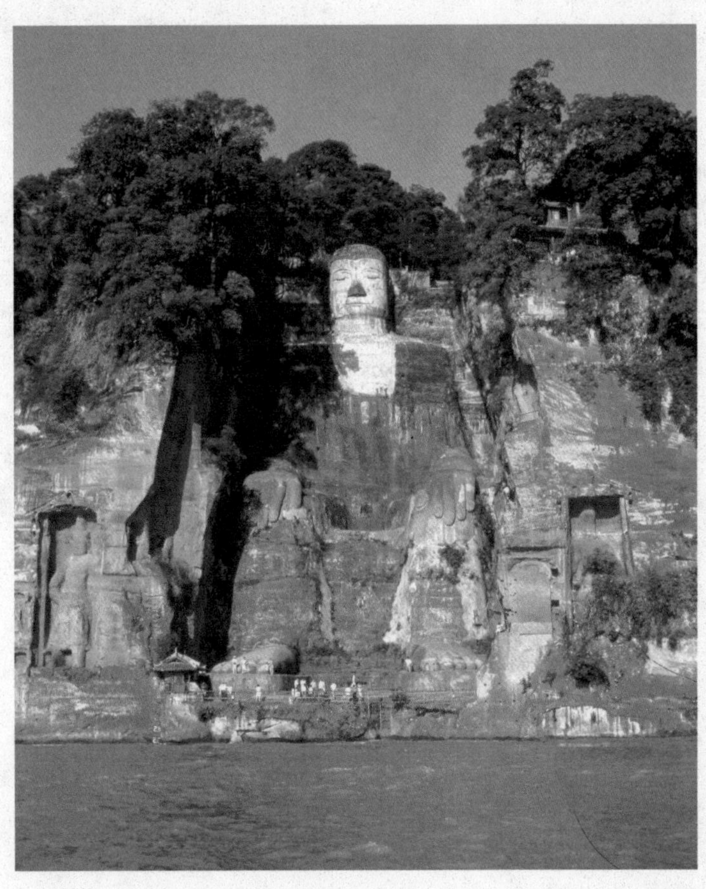

乐山大佛
The Giant Buddha of Leshan

小故事 Anecdote

据说，三江口水急浪高，唐朝僧人海通认为有恶龙在兴风作浪，他想造一个大佛镇住恶龙。于是，他到处化缘筹款，凿了这尊大佛。后人建了海师堂，来纪念这位大佛的创建者。

It is said that at the convergence of the three rivers the flow was torrential, so that Hai Tong, a monk in the Tang Dynasty, thought there must be an evil dragon living there to make trouble. So, he decided to make a giant Buddha to crush the evil dragon. He visited many places to raise funds and made this giant Buddha. People of later generations built the Hall of Master Hai to commemorate him.

你知道吗 Do you know

乐山大佛赤裸的脚背上可围坐100多人。

The back of the bare foot of the Giant Buddha of Leshan can seat over 100 persons.

1. 乐山大佛的脚背
   The back of the bare foot of the Giant Buddha of Leshan
2. 大佛旁的石梯
   The stone stairs by the Giant Buddha

大佛是一尊高70.8米的石刻弥勒佛坐像，头高14.7米，宽10米，肩宽28米，眼长3.3米，耳长7米，手指长8.3米，发髻1,021个。大佛造型优美，气势雄伟。

The 70.8-m-tall statue of the Laughing Buddha is in a sitting posture. Its head is 14.7 m high and 10 m wide; its shoulders are 28 m wide; its eyes 3.3 m long, its ears seven meters long and its fingers 8.3 m long. There are 1,021 chignons.

普陀山
Mount Putuo

普陀山是浙江省东部舟山群岛中的一座山岛，是中国四大佛教胜地之一，有"海天佛国"之称，也是著名的旅游胜地。

Mount Putuo is an island of mountains among the Zhoushan Archipelago east of Zhejiang Province. It is one of the four holy places of Buddhism and has a reputation of being "a Buddhist land of the sea and the sky". It is also a famous tourist spot.

普陀山上的法雨禅寺
Fayu Temple, Mount Putuo

你知道吗 Do you know

每到观音菩萨的生日，都要举行隆重的佛教仪式，有许多善男信女来这里烧香，非常热闹。

A grand Buddhist ceremony is held every year to celebrate the Goddess of Mercy's birthday, during which thousands of devotees come to burn incense.

小资料 Data

公元916年，日本僧人从五台山请观音像回国。经过普陀山时，被大风所阻，于是就在普陀山紫竹林建了一座名为"不肯去观音院"的寺庙。从此以后，普陀山成为供奉观音菩萨的佛山。

In 916, after paying homage to Mount Wutai in Shanxi Province a Japanese monk was shipping the statue of Goddess of Mercy to Japan. When he arrived at Mount Putuo, he was blocked by a strong wind, and so he built a temple named "the Goddess of Mercy Temple of Not Willing to Leave" in the Purple Bamboo Forest on Mount Putuo. From then on, Mount Putuo became a Buddhist mountain for worshipping the Goddess of Mercy.

普陀山是以山水优美著称的名山，山海相连，秀丽雄伟。

普陀山名胜古迹很多，以普济、法雨、慧济三寺为主的建筑群最具代表性，其中普济寺最大。

普济寺

普济寺始建于宋朝，是供奉观音菩萨的主刹，建筑总面积11,000多平方米。寺内有大圆通殿、天王殿、藏经殿、钟鼓楼等。

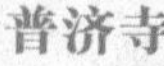

1. 普陀山香客众多
   Many people worshipped at the temple on Mount Putuo.
2. 普陀山上的南海观音
   South sea's Goddess of Mercy, Mount Putuo

There are many scenic spots and historical sites on Mount Putuo. A typical example is the building complex mainly consisting of the Puji Temple, the Fayu Temple and the Huiji Temple. Puji Temple is the biggest.

The Puji Temple

The Puji Temple, first built in the Song Dynasty, is the main monastery for worshipping the Goddess of Mercy. It covers a floor space of more than 11,000 m^2. In it there are the Great Hall of Flexibility, the Hall of Celestial King, the Tripitaka Hall, the Tower of Bell and Drum, etc.

2

九华山
Mount Jiuhua

九华山位于安徽省西南部，是中国四大佛教名山之一，有“香火甲天下”、“东南第一山”之称，进香朝拜的中外游客终年络绎不绝。

Mount Jiuhua, situated in the southwest of Anhui Province, is one of the four famous Buddhist mountains in China, with a reputation of being “the busiest pilgrimage place under heaven” and “the first mountain in the Southeast”. It attracts numerous domestic and foreign tourists to burn incense and worship all year round.

九华山之巅天台正顶
The Heavenly Terrace Peak, Mount Jiuhua

1. 天台寺的和尚在十王峰上打坐
   A monk from Heavenly Terrace Temple meditates on the Peak of Ten Kings.
2. 化城寺门前
   In front of the Huacheng Temple
3. 肉身殿
   The Treasure Hall of Corporeal Body
4. 百岁宫的海玉肉身
   The corporeal body of Haiyu at the One-Hundred-Year Palace

九华山自然风光十分秀美，有99座山峰，以天台、莲华、天柱、十王等九峰最为雄伟，主峰十王峰海拔1,342米。

九华山气候宜人，环境优美，被称为"佛国仙城"。有化城寺、肉身宝殿、百岁宫等大小寺庙84座，大小佛像6,800多尊，是善男信女的朝拜圣地和旅游避暑胜地。

化城寺

化城寺是九华山的主寺，公元781年被辟为地藏道场，当时皇帝赐匾额"化城寺"。寺内藏有许多经文，是国家稀有文物。

肉身宝殿

相传肉身宝殿藏有地藏菩萨的肉身，殿内有许多佛教珍贵文物。

百岁宫

百岁宫又叫万年寺，是为了供奉无瑕禅师的真身而修建的。

 你知道吗 Do you know

九华山有棵凤凰古松，已经生长了1,400多年，是九华山一大胜景。

There is an old pine tree on Mount Jiuhua that has lived for over 1,400 years.

Mount Jiuhua has very beautiful natural scenery and 99 peaks, among which the nine peaks of the Heavenly Terrace, Lotus Glory, Heavenly Pillar, Ten Kings, and so on are the most magnificent. The main Peak of Ten Kings is 1,342 m above sea level.

Mount Jiuhua has pleasant weather and a graceful environment, and is reputed to be "a Buddhist land of the immortals". There are 84 temples, such as the Huacheng Temple, the Treasure Hall of Corporeal Body, and the One-Hundred-Year Palace, and over 6,800 Buddhist statues. It is a holy place for devotees to worship and also a summer resort for tourists.

Huacheng Temple

Huacheng Temple is the main temple of Mount Jiuhua. In 781, it was opened as a place where Taoist rites of the Earth Buddha were performed. At that time, the emperor granted a horizontal board bearing the characters of "Huacheng Temple". A large collection of rare Buddhist scriptures is housed in the temple.

Treasure Hall of Corporeal Body

It is said that the corporeal body of the Earth Buddha is kept in this hall, along with many precious Buddhist cultural relics.

The One-Hundred-Year Palace

The One-Hundred-Year Palace is also named the Ten-Thousand-Year Temple. It was built for enshrining the body of the Zen Master of Wuxia.

3

4

小资料 Data

古新罗国(今朝鲜)高僧金乔觉来九华山修行，99岁圆寂，3年肉身不烂，人们认为他是地藏菩萨转世。从此，九华山成为地藏菩萨的道场。

In ancient times, Jin Qiaojue, an eminent monk from what is today's North Korea came to Mount Jiuhua to cultivate his way. At the age of 99, he passed away, but his body remained intact for three years, so he was respected as the incarnation of the Earth Buddha. From then on, Mount Jiuhua became a place where Taoist rites of the Earth Buddha were performed.

无瑕禅师来九华山修行时才26岁，长年以野果、泉水为生，活到126岁，坐化而死。死后3年，身体保存完好。现在，殿内所供奉的是无瑕禅师的真身。

The Zen Master Wuxia was only 26 years old when he came to Mount Jiuhua to practice Buddhism. For many years he lived on wild fruits and spring water. He was sitting cross-legged when he died at the age of 126. His body was kept intact three years after he died. Now, the palace enshrines the real body of the Zen Master of Wuxia.

五台山
Mount Wutai

五台山位于山西省境内，是中国四大佛教胜地之一。建筑古朴，气候凉爽，是旅游、避暑的好地方。

Mount Wutai, situated in Shanxi Province, is one of the four famous holy places of Buddhism in China. The buildings are old and simple and the weather is cool. It is a good place for summer relaxation.

1

小资料 Data

"灵峰胜境"菩萨顶有一座"滴水殿"，有趣的是，不管天晴还是下雨，宝殿四檐都是雨珠下滴，天长日久，檐台的石条上被滴出一排排深坑。

On the Peak of the Bodhisattva, there is a "Hall of Dripping Water". The funny thing is that, no matter whether it is sunny or rainy, there is always rain dripping from the eaves of the hall, and after a long time a row of holes appears in the stone slates.

2

五台山有五座高大的山峰，它们是北台叶斗峰、东台望海峰、西台挂月峰、南台锦绣峰、中台翠岩峰。最高峰是叶斗峰，海拔3,000米以上。

五台山寺庙很多，共有58座。最著名的有5处，分别是塔院寺、显通寺、殊像寺、罗睺寺和菩萨顶。它们的建筑非常有特色，是中国古代建筑的精华。

五台山是供奉文殊菩萨的佛山。

显通寺

显通寺是五台山历史最久、规模最大的寺庙。建于汉代，人们称它为“祖寺”。

Mount Wutai has five high and grand peaks: Northern Peak of Yedou, Eastern Peak of Viewing the Sea, Western Peak of Hanging Moon, Southern Peak of Charm and Middle Peak of Green Rock. The highest peak is the Peak of Yedou, more than 3,000 m above sea level.

1. 殊像寺内的文殊像
Bodhisattva Manjusri, the Temple of the Statue of Manjusri
2. 五台山寺庙林立
Mount Wutai has many temples.

你知道吗 Do you know

峨眉山、普陀山、九华山、五台山被称为中国四大佛教名山。

Mount Emei, Mount Putuo, Mount Jiuhua and Mount Wutai are the four famous mountains of Buddhism in China.

小知识 Knowledge

菩萨顶有个"万人斋"用的大铜锅。猜猜看，这大铜锅究竟有多大？据说，僧人吃过饭后，锅底的锅巴要用大黄牛拉着犁来耕呢！

There is a huge copper pot for "ten thousand people's meal" in the Temple of the Bodhisattva. Can you imagine how big the pot is? It is said that after monks finished their meals, the rice crust left in the pot needed to be ploughed by a big ox!

1. 显通寺铜殿内的万佛铜像
The "ten thousand bronze Buddha statues" at the Temple of Revealing Comprehension
2. 显通寺
The Temple of Revealing Comprehension

There are altogether 58 temples on Mount Wutai. Among them, the most famous are the Temple of Pagoda Courtyard, the Temple of Revealing Comprehension, the Temple of the Statue of Manjusri, the Temple of Luohou (name of a constellation that astrologers believe can dominate the fate of humans) and the Temple of the Bodhisattva. The architecture of the temples is distinctive and they are the essence of Chinese ancient architecture.

Mount Wutai is where Bodhisattva Manjusri is enshrined and worshipped.

The Temple of Revealing Comprehension

The Temple of Revealing Comprehension is the biggest temple with the longest history on Mount Wutai. Built in the Han Dynasty (206 BC – 220 AD), it is called "the ancestral temple".

莫高窟
The Mogao Grottoes

莫高窟又叫“千佛洞”，位于甘肃省敦煌东南25千米的鸣沙山东麓，是中国四大石窟之一，也是世界上最大、内容最多的佛教石窟群，现已被联合国列入世界文化遗产名录。

The Mogao Grottoes, also called "Cave of Ten Thousand Buddhas", located on the eastern foot of the Mingsha Mountain 25 km southeast of Dunhuang in Gansu Province, is one of the four great grottoes in China and also the largest Buddhist grotto. UNESCO lists it as one of the world cultural heritage sites.

莫高窟第428窟内的精美塑像及壁画
The exquisite sculptures and murals of the Mogao Grottoes (Grottoes No. 428)

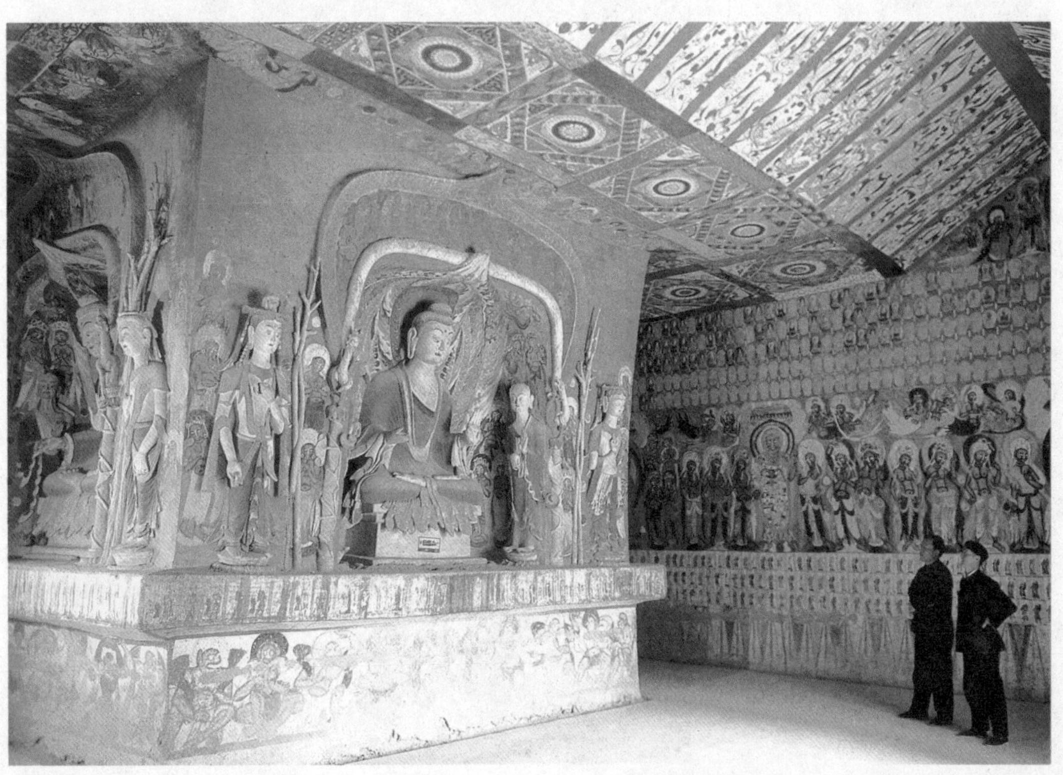

莫高窟始建于公元366年，南北长1,610米。现有洞窟492个，壁画45,000多平方米，彩塑2,400多尊。

石窟大小不等，塑像高矮不一，大的雄伟浑厚，小的精巧玲珑。壁画精美绝伦，内容多为佛经故事。艺术造诣精深，想像力丰富，令人惊叹。

壁画虽然经过千百年的风沙侵蚀，但仍然色彩鲜艳，线条清晰，使人不得不赞叹古代艺术匠师们的精湛技艺和创造精神。

小资料 Data

洞窟中除了壁画和彩塑外，还有大量经卷、文书，为研究中国古代的政治、经济、军事、文化、艺术、宗教、民族史等提供了宝贵的资料。

Apart from murals and colorful statues, there is a large number of scriptures and documents that provide precious information for researching politics, economics, military affairs, culture, arts, religion and the national history of ancient China.

如果把莫高窟的壁画连接起来，可长达25千米。壁画不仅体现了中国的民族风格，而且吸取了印度、希腊、伊朗等国古代艺术之长，是东西方文化的结晶。

If one joins all the murals of the Mogao Grottoes together they stretch 25 km. The murals not only represent the national style of China but also absorb the advantages from the ancient arts of India, Greece and Persia, etc. It is the quintessence of both East and West cultures.

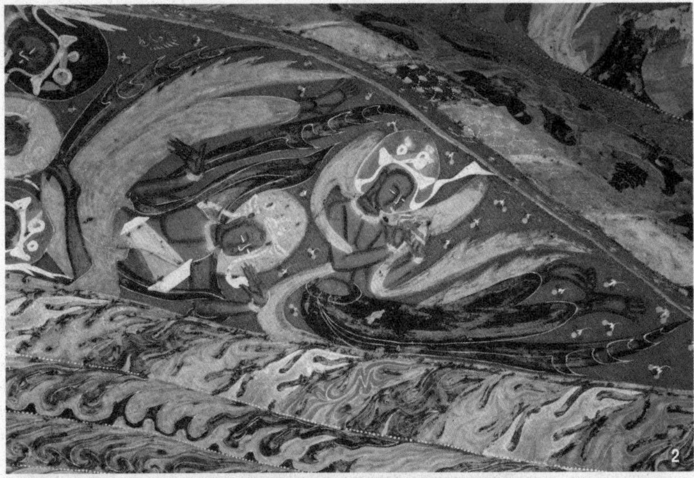

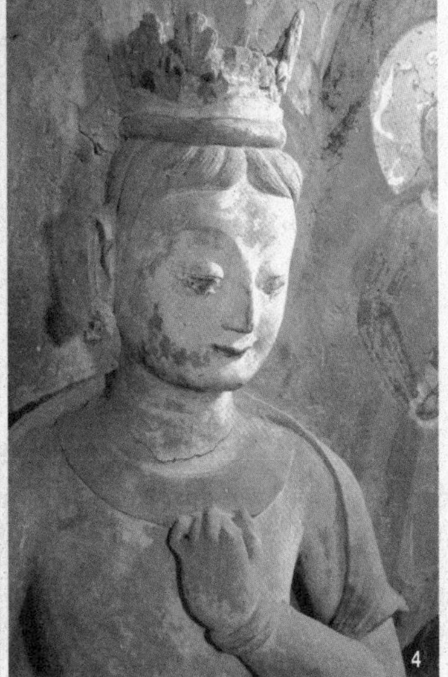

1. 三危山下的莫高窟外观
Mogao Grottoes at the foot of Sanwei Mountain
2. 西魏时的壁画飞天（249窟）
Painted during the Western Wei Dynasty (535 - 556 AD), the mural (Grotto No. 249) depicts the Buddhist paradise.
3. 17窟又称“藏经洞”。1900年窟内一小洞被发现藏有经卷、织绣等文物共50,000余件。图为窟内的壁画。
This mural was found in Grottoes No. 17, which is also called the "Cave Preserving Buddhist Scriptures". The cave once stored over 50,000 pieces of scriptures and embroideries in 1900 AD.
4. 隋代造像
The sculpture was created during the Sui Dynasty (581 - 618 AD).

The Mogao Grottoes, first built in 366 AD, extend 1,610 m from south to north. There are 492 caves and 45,000 m^2 of murals and over 2,400 statues in different colors.

The caves are different in size and the statues are varied in height. The big statues are grand and the small ones are refined. The murals are extremely exquisite and mainly describe the stories of Buddhist scriptures. Their high artistic attainment and the rich imagination astonish people.

Though the murals have gone through hundreds of years of sand storms, they still have bright colors and clear lines.

你知道吗 Do you know

中国有四大石窟，分别是甘肃省的敦煌莫高窟、河南省的龙门石窟、山西省的云冈石窟和甘肃省的麦积山石窟。

There are four great grottoes in China: the Mogao Grottoes of Dunhuang in Gansu Province, the Longmen Grottoes in Henan Province, the Yungang Grottoes in Shanxi Province and the Maijishan Grottoes in Gansu Province.

承德避暑山庄
The Summer Resort of Chengde

承德避暑山庄在河北省承德市北部山林中，是中国最著名的清代园林之一，现已被联合国列入世界文化遗产名录。

The Summer Resort, located in the mountain forest north of Chengde City in Hebei Province, is one of the most famous gardens of the Qing Dynasty, now listed by UNESCO as one of the world cultural heritage sites.

1

2

3

承德避暑山庄景色优美，气候凉爽。有山，有水，有林，有泉，是避暑的好地方。

山庄内的建筑是用青砖、青瓦建成的，主要建筑有正宫、松鹤斋、万壑松风、普乐寺、烟雨楼等。

The Summer Resort of Chengde has a beautiful scenery and pleasant weather. There are mountains, waterways, forests and springs. It is a good place for spending summers.

Buildings in the Summer Resort are built by using gray bricks and tiles. The main ones are the Main Palace, Pine-and-Crane Hall, Ten Thousand Valleys and Pine Wind, Temple of Universal Happiness and the Tower of Mist and Rain.

小资料 Data

清朝康熙皇帝为了团结北方少数民族，在承德附近建了一个木兰围场用于打猎，并为此兴建了一座行宫，因行宫周围山岭环绕，气候宜人，康熙皇帝便将行宫题名为"避暑山庄"。

Emperor Kangxi (1662–1723 AD) of the Qing Dynasty built a royal hunting ground with wooden fence near Chengde for uniting the national minorities in Northern China. And because of this, he built an imperial palace for short stays when away from the capital. As it was encircled by mountains, and with a pleasant climate, Emperor Kangxi designated it a "summer resort".

你知道吗 Do you know

承德避暑山庄的周围都是用石头砌成的宫墙，长10千米，是中国最长的宫墙。

The stone wall surrounding the Summer Resort of Chengde is 10 km long, the longest imperial wall in China.

1. 金山亭
   Jinshan Tower
2. 烟雨楼
   The Tower of Mist and Rain
3. 避暑山庄外的普陀宗乘之庙
   The Putuo Temple outside of Chengde Summer Resort

长 城
The Great Wall

长城是世界七大奇观之一，是炎黄子孙血汗与智慧的结晶，也是中华民族坚毅、勤奋的象征。它以宏大的气势和壮美的英姿享誉世界，吸引着天下的游人，现已被联合国列入世界文化遗产名录。

The Great Wall, one of the seven wonders in the world, is the crystallization of the blood, sweat and wisdom of the Chinese nation and also a sign of Chinese people's persistence and diligence. It is known for its incomparable grandeur, attracting tourists from all over the world. UNESCO lists it as one of the world cultural heritage sites.

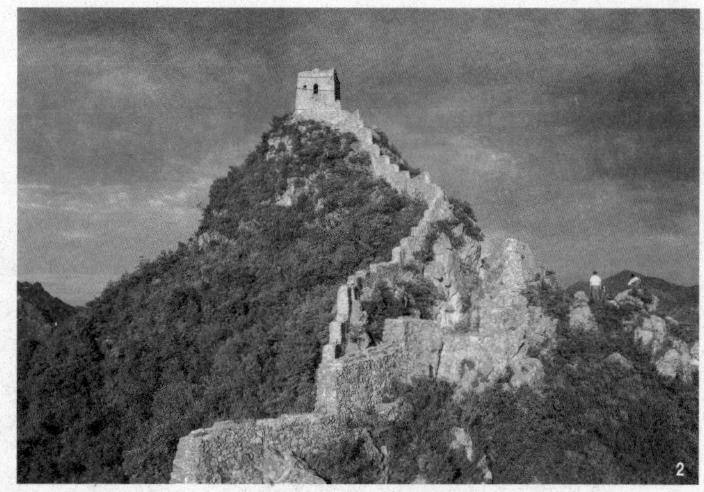

1. 金山岭长城
   Jinshanling Great Wall
2. 司马台长城
   Simatai Great Wall

八达岭长城

八达岭长城位于北京西北部，它依山而筑，城墙高7.8米，宽5.8米，可以同时让五六匹马并行通过。登上八达岭长城远眺，山峦叠嶂，雄伟壮观。

居庸关

居庸关在北京的西北部，它修筑在海拔800多米的山上，异常险峻。

1. 八达岭长城
   Baidaling Great Wall
2. 居庸关云台
   The gate tower of Juyong Pass
3. 嘉峪关
   Jiayu Pass
4. 山海关
   Shanhai Pass

嘉峪关

嘉峪关在甘肃省境内，是长城最西端的关隘，有"天下雄关"之称。

山海关

山海关位于河北省秦皇岛市境内，是万里长城的第一关。

Badaling Great Wall

Badaling Great Wall, lying in the northwest of Beijing, was built along the mountain ridges. It is 7.8 m tall and 5.8 m wide, so that five or six horses

could pass through side by side. Standing on the Badaling Great Wall, one can see mountains undulating splendidly into the far distance.

Juyong Pass

Juyong Pass, situated in the northwest of Beijing, is 800 m above the sea level and is considered a very precipitous and dangerous place.

Jiayu Pass

Jiayu Pass, in Gansu Province, is the western terminus of the Great Wall and is reputed to be "the most impregnable pass in the world".

Shanhai Pass

Shanhai Pass, situated in the city of Qinhuangdao, Hebei Province, is the first pass of the Great Wall.

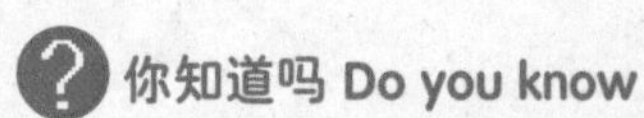

嘉峪关、居庸关、山海关是万里长城上的三座重要的关隘。

Jiayu Pass, Juyong Pass and Shanhai Pass are the three important passes of the Great Wall.

4

秦始皇陵与兵马俑坑
The Qinshihuang Mausoleum and Terracotta Warriors and Horses

1

秦始皇陵与兵马俑坑在陕西省临潼县境内，是目前世界上最大的帝王陵墓博物馆，号称“世界第八奇观”，现已被联合国列入世界文化遗产名录。

The Qinshihuang Mausoleum and Terracotta Warriors and Horses, situated in Lintong County of Shaanxi Province, is the largest imperial mausoleum museum in the world and is often called "the eighth wonder in the world". UNESCO lists it as one of the world cultural heritage sites.

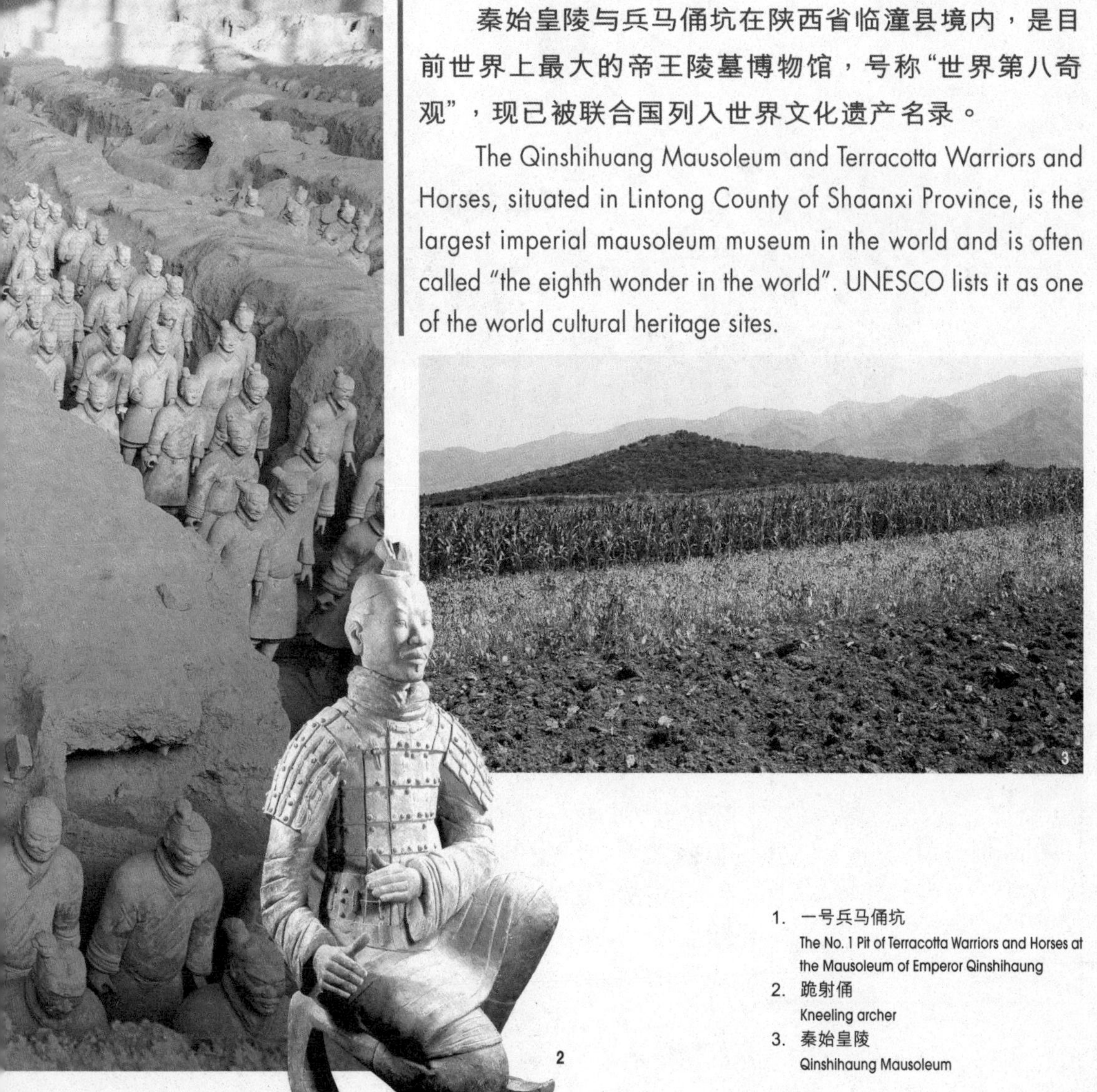

1. 一号兵马俑坑
   The No. 1 Pit of Terracotta Warriors and Horses at the Mausoleum of Emperor Qinshihaung
2. 跪射俑
   Kneeling archer
3. 秦始皇陵
   Qinshihaung Mausoleum

1

2

3

4

你知道吗 Do you know

秦始皇陵墓内有无数奇珍异宝。为防止盗墓，墓门上装有机关，并将修墓的工匠和送葬的宫女全部活埋在墓道里。

There are numerous rare treasures and jewelry items in the Qinshihuang Mausoleum. To deter grave robbers, the mausoleum gate was fixed with tricky gears and all the craftsmen who built the mausoleum and maids who joined the funeral procession were buried alive in the path leading to the mausoleum.

秦始皇陵是秦始皇13岁当皇帝后，动用70多万人，花了36年的时间建成的。陵墓长515米，宽55.05米，高79米，就像金字塔一样。

在秦始皇陵东侧1,500米的地方有三个举世闻名的兵马俑坑。其中"一号坑"最大，东西长230米，南北宽62米，深5米。坑内排列着许多与真人真马一样高大的兵马俑，包括步兵、骑兵和车兵。还有多种兵器，这些兵器埋在地下已经有2,000多年，到现在还寒光闪闪。

Work began on the Qinshihuang Mausoleum when the emperor ascended to the throne at the age of 13. It took over 700,000 laborers 36 years to finish the pyramid-like building, which is 515 m long, 55.05 m wide and 79 m high.

At a point some 1,500 m to the east of the Qinshihuang Mausoleum there are three pits containing terracotta warriors and horses, among which "the Number One Pit" is the biggest, 230 m long from east to west, 62 m wide from south to north and five meters deep. Displayed in it are thousands of life-size terracotta warriors and horses, including foot, horse and chariot soldiers. Their weapons still gleam though they have been buried for more than 2,000 years.

1. 武士俑
Head of terracotta warrior
2. 将军俑
Terracotta General
3. 战袍俑
Terracotta warrior in battle uniform
4. 铜车马
Bronze chariot and horses
5. 武士与战车俑
Terracotta warriors and horses

长江三峡
The Three Gorges of the Yangtze River

长江三峡西起重庆市的白帝城，东到湖北省的南津关，由瞿塘峡、巫峡、西陵峡三段峡谷和其间两个宽谷组成。全长193千米。

The Three Gorges of the Yangtze River, starting from Baidicheng of Chongqing in the west and extending to Nanjinguan of Hubei Province in the east, comprise Qutang Gorge, Wuxia Gorge and Xiling Gorge and the two wide valleys between them. The total length is 193 km.

长江三峡以其险峻的地形、绮丽的风光、磅礴的气势和众多的名胜古迹而成为世界著名的旅游胜地，是中国的旅游热点。

瞿塘峡

瞿塘峡雄伟险峻，全长8千米，江面最窄的地方不到100米，最宽的不超过150米，有“天堑”之称。在这里有许多风景名胜，如铁锁关、孟良梯、倒吊和尚等。

巫峡

巫峡幽深秀丽，全长40千米，是三峡中狭长而整齐的峡谷。巫峡南北两岸有12座山峰，千姿百态，非常优美。

巫峡名胜古迹较多，以孔明碑和神女峰最为著名。

西陵峡

西陵峡滩多水急，全长约有75千米，是三峡中最长的峡谷。著名的景点有兵书宝剑峡、牛肝马肺峡、黄牛峡、灯影峡、青滩、泄滩、崆岭滩等。当地有歌谣唱道：青滩泄滩不算滩，崆岭才算鬼门关。

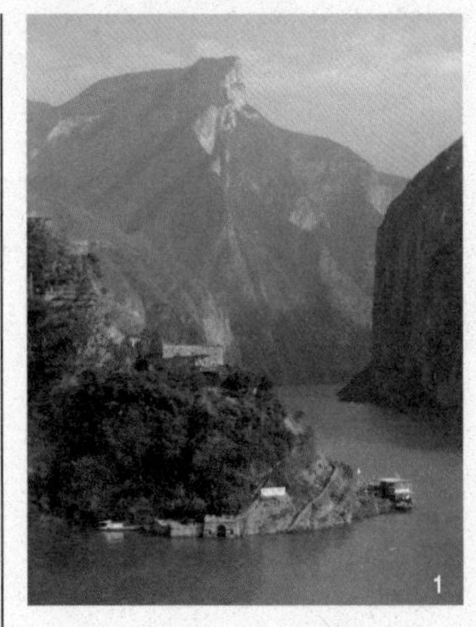

1. 瞿塘峡
Qutang Gorge
2. 狭长幽深的巫峡
The deep and narrow Wuxia Gorge

The Three Gorges of the Yangtze River has become a world famous tourist hot spot in China because of its precipitous terrain, beautiful scenery, incomparable grandeur and numerous scenic spots and historical sites.

Qutang Gorge

The grand and dangerous Qutang Gorge is eight kilometers long. The narrowest place is less than 100 m wide and the widest place is no more than 150 m, therefore it has a name of "chasm". There are many scenic spots, such as Iron Lock Pass, Meng Liang Ladder, Monk Hanging Upside Down, and so on.

1. 巫峡
   Wuxia Gorge
2. 西陵峡
   Xiling Gorge

Wuxia Gorge

The Wuxia Gorge, deep and graceful, is 40 km long and is a narrow, long and the most orderly gorge among the three gorges, lined on its northern and southern banks by 12 peaks.

There are lots of scenic spots and historical sites, the most famous being the Kong Ming Tablet and the Goddess Peak.

Xiling Gorge

The Xiling Gorge has many shoals and a torrential current. At 75 km, it is the longest gorge of the three gorges. There are many famous scenic spots, such as the Gorge of War Books and Treasured Sword, the Gorge of Ox's Liver and Horse's Lung, the Gorge of the Ox, the Lamplight Gorge, the Green Shoal, the Xie Shoal and the Kongling Shoal, etc. A folk song goes like this: the Green Shoal and the Xie Shoal can't count as shoals; the Kongling Shoal is the gate to hell.

九寨沟
Jiuzhaigou (Nine-Village Valley)

五彩池
Five-Color Pond

九寨沟位于四川省北部，处于岷山山脉之中，是由彩池、瀑布、森林、雪山构成的自然风景，被称为“童话世界”，已被联合国列入世界自然遗产名录。

Jiuzhaigou, situated in the north of Sichuan Province and as part of the Min Mountains, comprises colorful ponds, waterfalls, forests and snow-capped mountains. UNESCO designates this “fairyland” as one of the world natural heritage sites.

九寨沟是一条纵深50千米的山沟谷地，四周是高耸的雪峰，谷地有茂密的原始森林。在这里有100多个美丽的高山湖泊(当地人称为"海子")，最有名的是长海、五彩池、镜海等。湖水清澈见底，湖底各种颜色的沉积物和水藻，使湖水呈黄、橙、蓝、绿等多种颜色，五彩缤纷，非常迷人。人们把它叫做"人间仙境"。

瀑布是九寨沟的一绝，最壮观的是诺日朗瀑布，其次是珍珠滩瀑布和树正瀑布。

小知识 Knowledge

因为这里有九座古老的藏族村寨，九寨沟因此而得名。

There are nine old Tibetan villages in the valley, hence the name.

Jiuzhaigou is a 50-km-long valley surrounded by towering snow-capped mountains. In the valley there are dense primitive forests. There are more than 100 beautiful lakes in the high mountains (local people call them *haizi*), among which the Long Lake, the Five-Color Pond and the Mirror Lake are the most famous. The lakes are crystal clear so that one can see the bottom. The deposits of various colors and algae at the bottom of the lakes make the water look yellow, orange, blue and green.

The waterfalls are one of the unique features of Jiuzhaigou. The most splendid one is Nuorilang Waterfall, next to which are the Waterfall of Pearl Shoal and the Shuzheng Waterfall.

1. 秋天的五花海岸上
   The Wuhua Coast in autumn
2. 诺日朗瀑布
   Nuorilang Waterfall
3. 雪山下的藏族村寨
   The Tibetan village at the foot of the snow mountains

桂林山水
The Scenery of Guilin

桂林山水以桂林市为中心，北起兴安灵渠，南至阳朔，由漓江一水相连，集“山清、水秀、洞奇、石美”四绝于一体，有“桂林山水甲天下”的美称。

The unique scenery of Guilin, with Guilin City in the center, starts from Lingqu of Xing'an in the north and extends to Yangshuo and is connected by the Li River. It has four unique features of "verdant mountains, limpid waters, special caves and beautiful rocks" that enjoy worldwide reputation.

阳朔风光
A splendid view of Yangshuo

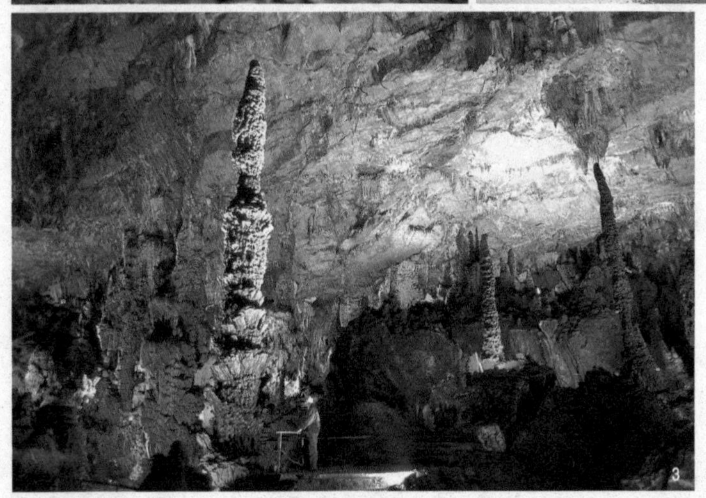

独秀峰

独秀峰是桂林十大景观之一。要爬上山峰的顶端，必须经过306级蜿蜒的石阶。山崖上，有历代文人题写的诗句，具有一定的历史和艺术价值。

象鼻山

象鼻山在漓江西岸，它的形状就像一头巨象站在江边伸长鼻子喝水，形象逼真。

七星岩

七星岩在漓江东岸，是桂林最著名的岩洞，分上、中、下三层。洞内有地下河、地下画廊，以及许多石钟乳、石笋、石柱等。

漓江

桂林漓江风景区是世界上规模最大的岩溶山水风景区。这里奇峰对峙，飞瀑连连，峰峦叠秀，碧水如镜，景色无比秀美。

1. 独秀峰
   The Peak of Unmatched Beauty
2. 象鼻山
   The Hill of Elephant Trunk
3. 七星岩
   Seven-Star Cave
4. 漓江两岸的渔夫至今仍用"鱼鹰"捕鱼
   The fishermen of the Li River are still relied upon kingfishers to catch their preys today.

The Peak of Unmatched Beauty

The Peak of Unmatched Beauty is one of the ten major attractions in Guilin. One must climb the winding 306 stone steps to reach the top. On the cliff there are poems written by literati of each dynasty, which are now of some historical and artistic value.

The Hill of Elephant Trunk

The Hill of Elephant Trunk, on the western bank of the Li River, looks like an elephant dipping its trunk to drink from the nearby river.

Seven-Star Cave

The Seven-Star Cave, on the eastern bank of the Li River, is the most famous cave in Guilin, with three layers of upper, middle and lower. There is an underground river, an underground gallery and many stalactites, stalagmites and stone pillars, etc.

The Li River

The Li River Scenic Spot of Guilin is the largest karst scenic spot in the world. There are grotesque peaks standing facing each other, along with flying waterfalls and waters as clear as a mirror.

小知识 Knowledge

桂林山水位于石灰岩分布地区，这里山多、洞多、水也多，有"无山不洞、无洞不奇"的赞句。

Guilin's uniqueness is due to its geological formation—the limestone that produces myriads of mountains, caves and waterways.

路南石林
The Stone Forest of Lunan

路南石林位于云南省石林彝族自治县。这里到处是奇峰异洞，危崖峭壁，是中国重要的风景名胜区。

The Stone Forest of Lunan, situated in the Shilin Yi Autonomous County, is an important and famous scenic spot. Grotesque peaks, unusual caves and sheer cliffs can be found everywhere.

路南石林主要景区有大石林、小石林、外石林等。石林的石峰千姿百态，巧夺天工，数量奇多，为世界罕见。石峰之间还有小湖泊、地下溶洞、地下暗河等。

小知识 Knowledge

路南石林，远看就像一片"岩石之林"，是石灰岩经过几千万年的流水溶蚀而形成的。

The Stone Forest of Lunan is like "a forest of stones" seen from afar. It was formed from limestone being eroded for millions of years by flowing water.

阿诗玛峰

这是小石林中的阿诗玛峰。你看它像不像一位美丽的少女？

万年灵芝

外石林中的"万年灵芝"，高达10米。

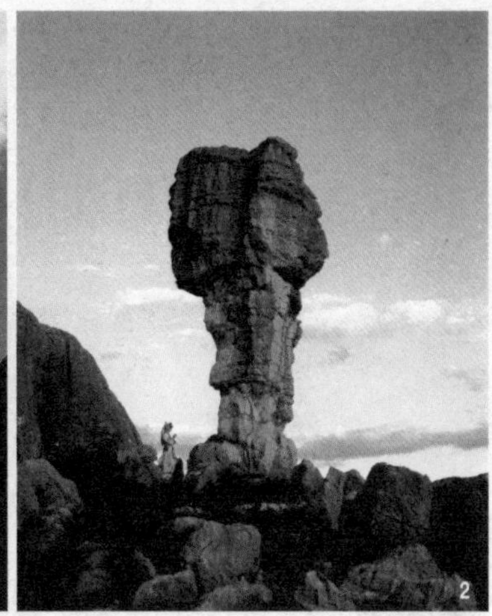

1. "阿诗玛"峰
   Ashima Peak
2. "万年灵芝"
   Ten-Thousand-Year Glossy Ganoderma

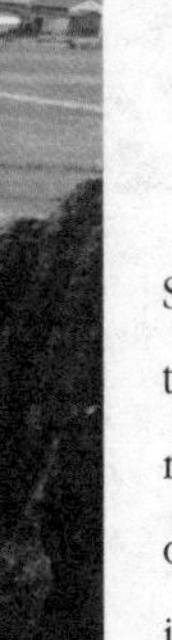

The main attractions are the Big Stone Forest, Small Stone Forest and the Outer Stone Forest. The large number of stone peaks are in a variety of shapes and postures, which is rare in the world. Among the stone peaks there are small lakes, underground caves and underground rivers.

Ashima Peak

This is the Ashima Peak in the Small Stone Forest. Doesn't it look like a beautiful girl?

Ten-Thousand-Year Glossy Ganoderma

This is the "Ten-Thousand-Year Glossy Ganoderma" in the Outer Stone Forest, which is 10 m tall.

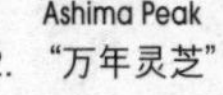

你知道吗 Do you know

每年农历六月廿四日的火把节，附近的彝族群众都会从四面八方汇集到石林来欢庆佳节。白天举行摔跤、爬杆、斗牛等比赛活动，夜晚则燃起熊熊篝火，耍龙、舞狮、表演民族歌舞。"阿细跳月"、"大三弦舞"是最受欢迎的传统节目。

On the Torchlight Festival every June 24 of the lunar calendar, the Yi people nearby gather at the Stone Forest to celebrate. In the daytime, activities of wrestling, climbing poles, bullfighting and so on are held, while at night, people light a fire, perform dragon dances and lion dances, and sing folk songs. "Ah Xi Dancing by the Moonlight" and "Da San Xian Dancing" are the most popular traditional programs.

西双版纳
Xishuangbanna

西双版纳位于云南省南部，是国家重点自然保护区和风景名胜区。

Xishuangbanna, situated in the south of Yunnan Province, is a national key nature reserve and famous scenic spot.

1. 独木成林
   One tree is enough to make a forest.
2. 穿山甲
   Pangolin
3. 白猴
   White monkey
4. 狨猴
   Marmoset
5. 野象
   Wild elephants

西双版纳到处是茂密的原始森林，树木种类很多，有被称为“死亡之神”的箭毒木，有抗癌效果较好的美登木，有冲天而起的望天树等。

森林中有很多种类的动物，如孔雀、野象、金丝猴、犀牛、虎等。孔雀，经常展开它们漂亮的尾屏，欢迎来游玩的客人。

因此，西双版纳是中国著名的“动植物王国”。

西双版纳居住着许多少数民族，其中以傣族居多，他们的语言、生活习惯、服装各不相同，每到多姿多采的民族节日，西双版纳便成了欢乐的海洋，热闹非凡。

1. 附生树上的鹿角蕨
   Platycerium wallichii grows on the trees
2. 大花马铃
   Birthwort
3. 白腹锦鸡
   Lady Amherst's Pheasant
4. 孔雀
   Peacock
5. 泼水节
   Water-Sprinkling Festival

Dense primitive forests can be found everywhere in Xishuangbanna. There is a variety of trees, such as the curare tree, which has a name of "god of death", the Maytenus hookeri Loes which has good anti-cancer effect, and *Parashorea cathayensis*, which towers into the sky.

In the forests live various animals like peacocks, wild elephants, golden-

1

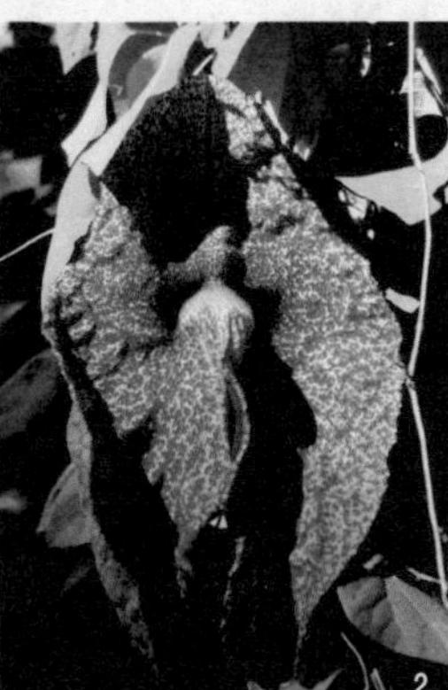
2

3

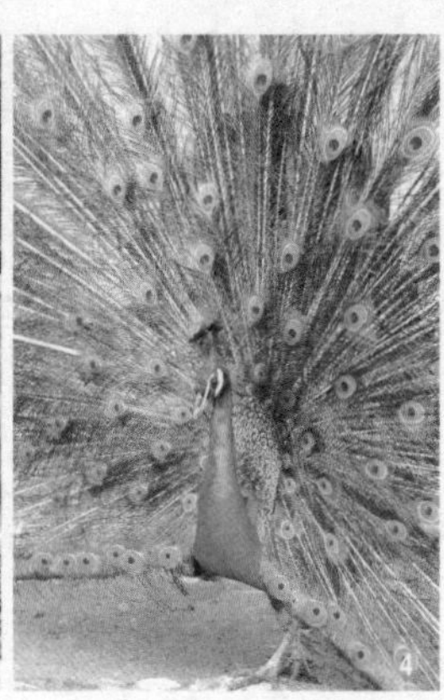
4

haired monkeys, rhinoceros, tigers and so on. Peacocks often spread their attractive tails to welcome tourists.

Xishuangbanna is home to many ethnic groups, the biggest of which is the Dai people. These ethnic groups have different languages, customs and costumes that enliven life in Xishuangbanna.

5

小知识 Knowledge

西双版纳拥有得天独厚的自然条件，常年平均温度为22℃，雨量充沛，终年温暖湿润，有利于各种植物的生长。

Xishuangbanna enjoys special favors from nature. The average temperature is 22°C, there is plentiful rain and it is warm and moist all year round, good for the growth of various plants.

附　录I APPENDIX I

中国之最
The Number Ones of China

- 中国面积最大的省区是新疆维吾尔自治区，有160万平方千米。
- 中国人口最多的省是河南省，到2000年11月1日止，有9,256万人。
- 中国人口最多的城市是上海市，到2000年11月1日止，有1,674万人。
- 中国最大的岛屿是台湾岛，面积3.576万平方千米。
- 中国最大的群岛是浙江省的舟山群岛，大小岛屿共670个，面积523平方千米。
- 中国最大的平原是东北平原，面积为35万平方千米。
- 中国最大的高原是青藏高原，它也是世界上地势最高的大高原，号称"世界屋脊"，面积有230万平方千米。
- 中国最高的山峰是珠穆朗玛峰，海拔为8,848.13米，也是世界上最高的山峰。
- 中国最大的盆地是塔里木盆地，面积约53万平方千米。
- 中国最大的沙漠是塔克拉玛干沙漠，面积33万平方千米。
- 中国最长的河流是长江，全长6,300千米，也是世界第三长河。
- 中国最大的淡水湖是鄱阳湖，面积约3,583平方千米。
- 中国最大的咸水湖和内陆湖是青海省的青海湖，面积4,583平方千米。
- 中国最深的湖泊是白头山上的天池，面积9.2平方千米，最深处312.7米。
- 中国海拔最低的湖泊是位于吐鲁番盆地的艾丁湖，湖面低于海平面155米，湖底最低处低于海平面283米。
- 中国最大的瀑布是贵州省的黄果树瀑布，瀑布宽30米，高50米，水量充沛。

- 中国年产量最大的油田是黑龙江省的大庆油田。
- 中国年产量最大的煤田是山西省的大同煤田。
- 中国年吞吐量最大的海港是上海港。
- 中国最热的地方是吐鲁番盆地，6、7、8三月平均气温达30℃，极端最高气温达49.6℃（1975年7月13日）。
- 中国最冷的地方是黑龙江省最北部的漠河乡，最低气温达零下52.3℃（1969年2月13日）。
- 中国年降水量最多的地方是台湾省基隆市的火烧寮，年平均降水量为6,557.8毫米。
- 中国年降水量最少的地方是新疆塔里木盆地东北部的托克逊（6.9mm），有时常年滴雨不下。
- 中国雾日最多的地区是四川省的峨眉山，每年雾日平均达327天（1953～1980年）。

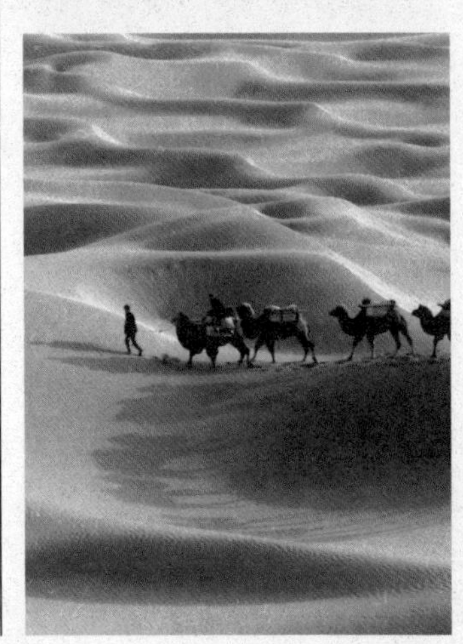

- The region with the biggest area is Xinjiang Uygur Autonomous Region. It covers 1.60 million km^2.
- The province with the largest population is Henan Province, with 92.56 million people by November 1, 2000.
- The city with the largest population is Shanghai, with 16.74 million people by November 1, 2000.
- The biggest island is Taiwan Island, with an area of 35,760 km^2.
- The biggest archipelago is the Zhoushan Archipelago in Zhejiang Province. It consists of 670 islands with total area of 523 km^2.
- The largest plain is the Northeast Plain, with an area of 350,000 km^2.
- The largest plateau is the Qinghai-Tibet Plateau, which is also the highest plateau in the world and reputed to be "the roof of the world". It has an area of 2.3 million km^2.
- The highest mountain is Qomolangma (Everest), with an altitude of 8,848.13 m, which is also the highest mountain in the world.
- The largest basin is the Tarim Basin, with an area of about 530,000 km^2.
- The biggest desert is the Taklamakan Desert, with an area of 330,000 km^2.
- The longest river is the Yangtze River, with a total length of 6,300 km, which is also the third longest river in the world.

- The biggest freshwater lake is Poyang Lake, with an area of about 3,583 km^2.
- The biggest salt lake and inland lake is Qinghai Lake in Qinghai Province, with an area of 4,583 km^2.
- The deepest lake is the Heavenly Pond on Baitou Mountain, with an area of 9.2 km^2 and maximum depth of 312.7 m.
- The lowest lake in China is Aiding Lake in the Turpan Basin, which is 155 m below sea level. The deepest place is 283 m below sea level.
- The largest waterfall is the Huangguoshu Waterfall in Guizhou Province, with a width of 30 m and a height of 50 m.
- The oilfield with the highest annual output is the Daqing Oilfield in Heilongjiang Province.
- The coal mine with the highest annual output is the Datong Coal Mine in Shanxi Province.
- The port with the largest annual handling capacity is the Shanghai Port.
- The hottest place is the Turpan Basin. The average temperature in June, July and August reaches 30°C. The highest temperature ever recorded was 49.6°C on July 13, 1975.
- The coldest place is Mohe Prefecture in the farthest north of Heilongjiang Province. The lowest temperature is -52.3°C on February 13, 1969.
- The place with the highest annual precipitation is Huoshaoliao in Jilong City of Taiwan, with an average annual precipitation of 6,557.8 mm.
- The place with the least annual precipitation is Toksun northeast of the Tarim Basin in Xinjiang. Sometimes there is no rain throughout the year.
- The place with the greatest number of foggy days is Mount Emei in Sichuan Province. There are an average 327 foggy days from 1953 to 1980.

附 录II APPENDIX II

中国所拥有的“世界遗产”
“The World Heritage” in China

名称 Name	所在省、市 Place	性质 Category
长城 The Great Wall	辽宁、河北、北京、山西、内蒙古、宁夏、陕西、甘肃 Liaoning, Hebei, Beijing, Shanxi, Inner Mongolia, Ningxia, Shaanxi, Gansu	世界文化遗产 World Cultural Heritage
明清故宫 The Palace Museum of the Ming and Qing Dynasties	北京市 Beijing	世界文化遗产 World Cultural Heritage
天坛 The Temple of Heaven	北京市 Beijing	世界文化遗产 World Cultural Heritage
周口店“北京猿人”遗址 “Peking Men” Ruins at Zhoukoudian	北京市 Beijing	世界文化遗产 World Cultural Heritage
颐和园 The Summer Palace	北京市 Beijing	世界文化遗产 World Cultural Heritage
承德避暑山庄及外八庙 The Summer Resort of Chengde and the Eight Outer Temples	河北省 Hebei Province	世界文化遗产 World Cultural Heritage
秦始皇陵及兵马俑坑 The Qinshihuang Mausoleum and the Qin Terracotta Warriors and Horses	陕西省 Shaanxi Province	世界文化遗产 World Cultural Heritage
拉萨布达拉宫 The Potala Palace of Lhasa	西藏自治区 Tibet Autonomous Region	世界文化遗产 World Cultural Heritage
敦煌莫高窟 The Mogao Grottoes of Dunhuang	甘肃省 Gansu Province	世界文化遗产 World Cultural Heritage
龙门石窟 The Longmen Grottoes	河南省 Henan Province	世界文化遗产 World Cultural Heritage
曲阜孔庙、孔林、孔府 The Confucius Temple, Confucius Forest, Confucius Mansion of Qufu	山东省 Shandong Province	世界文化遗产 World Cultural Heritage
泰山 Mount Tai	山东省 Shandong Province	世界自然和文化遗产 World Natural and Cultural Heritage

名称 Name	所在省、市 Place	性质 Category
平遥古城 The Ancient City of Pingyao	山西省 Shanxi Province	世界文化遗产 World Cultural Heritage
苏州古典园林 The Classical Gardens of Suzhou	江苏省 Jiangsu Province	世界文化遗产 World Cultural Heritage
明清皇家陵寝 The Imperial Mausoleums of the Ming and Qing Dynasties	河北省 Hebei Province	世界文化遗产 World Cultural Heritage
黄山 Mount Huangshan	安徽省 Anhui Province	世界自然和文化遗产 World Natural and Cultural Heritage
皖南古村落(西递—宏村) The Ancient Villages of South Anhui—Xidi and Hongcun	安徽省 Anhui Province	世界文化遗产 World Cultural Heritage
庐山 Mount Lushan	江西省 Jiangxi Province	世界文化遗产 World Cultural Heritage
武夷山 Mount Wuyi	福建省 Fujian Province	世界自然和文化遗产 World Natural and Cultural Heritage
武当山古建筑群 The Ancient Buildings of Mount Wudang	湖北省 Hubei Province	世界文化遗产 World Cultural Heritage
武陵源 Wulingyuan	湖南省 Hunan Province	世界自然遗产 World Natural Heritage
峨眉山—乐山大佛 Mount Emei and the Giant Buddha of Leshan	四川省 Sichuan Province	世界自然和文化遗产 World Natural and Cultural Heritage
黄龙风景区 The Huanglong Scenic Spot	四川省 Sichuan Province	世界自然遗产 World Natural Heritage
九寨沟 Jiuzhaigou	四川省 Sichuan Province	世界自然遗产 World Natural Heritage
大足石刻 The Dazu Grottoes	重庆市 Chongqing	世界文化遗产 World Cultural Heritage
丽江古城 The Ancient City of Lijiang	云南省 Yunnan Province	世界文化遗产 World Cultural Heritage
都江堰—青城山 The Dujiang Weir and Mount Qingcheng	四川省 Sichuan Province	世界文化遗产 World Cultural Heritage
云冈石窟 The Yungang Grottoes	山西省 Shanxi Province	世界文化遗产 World Cultural Heritage
三江并流 Three Parallel Rivers	云南省 Yunnan Province	世界自然遗产 World Natural Heritage
高句丽王城、王陵及贵族墓葬 Capital Cities and Tombs of the ancient Koguryo Kingdom	吉林省 Jilin Province	世界文化遗产 World Cultural Heritage
昆曲 Kunqu Opera	源于江苏省 Originated in Jiangsu Province	人类口头遗产和非物质遗产代表作 Masterpieces of the Oral and Intangible Heritage of Humanity

再版后记

Postscript for New Edition

《中国历史常识》、《中国地理常识》和《中国文化常识》于2002年1月与海外广大华裔青少年读者见面，及时缓解了海外华文教学辅助读物短缺的局面，并以其通俗易懂、生动活泼的编写风格受到了社会各界的热烈欢迎和好评。

由于初版时间比较仓促，三本书中尚存在一些不尽完善之处，诸位作者与编辑本着精益求精、认真负责的态度，对书中的某些内容和数据进行了全新的修订，以求进一步完善；全书并以中、英文对照再版。在修订再版工作中，潘兆明、杨伯震两位教授在百忙之中审读书稿并提出了许多宝贵意见，对我们的再版工作给予了大力支持和热情帮助，对此，我们谨表诚挚的谢意。

书中考虑不周或疏漏之处，期盼广大读者不吝赐正，以供今后再修订时参考。

编者

2004年9月

Common Knowledge about Chinese History, *Common Knowledge about Chinese Geography*, *Common Knowledge about Chinese Culture* were published in January 2002 and are now available to overseas young readers of Chinese origin. This has helped meet the demand for reference material for Chinese teaching abroad. The plain language and lively way of writing are both acclaimed by the general reading public.

There are places in the first edition of the three books for improvement. The authors and editors have carefully revised the books and updated some data and content. This edition is printed in bilingual format. Professor Pan Zhaoming and Yang Bozhen have, despite their own busy schedule, read the books and gave very valuable comments. We are most grateful to them for their time and support.

In case of any error or omission, please let us know. They will be used as reference for the next edition.

Compilers

September 2004

主编　焦华富
副主编　洪允智
编写人员　焦华富　方觉曙　李俊峰　赵春雨
责任编辑　金　红
英文编辑　林美琪
美术编辑　阮永贤　刘玉瑜

Chief Compiler : Jiao Huafu
Deputy Chief Compiler : Hong Yunzhi
Writers : Jiao Huafu, Fang Jueshu, Li Junfeng, Zhao Chunyu
Executive Editor : Jin Hong
English Editor : Maggie Lam
Designer : Yuen Wing Yin, Lau Yuk Yu

中国地理常识

图书在版编目(CIP)数据

中国地理常识/焦华富主编.—香港：香港中国旅游出版社，2004.9
ISBN 962-8746-48-0
I. 中…　II. 焦…　III. 地理—中国—儿童读物　IV. K92—49
中国版本图书馆CIP数据核字(2001)第081773号
出版：香港中国旅游出版社(中国 · 香港)
电话：(852)2561 8001
2004年9月第3版/2004年9月第1次印刷
印制：香港美雅印刷制本有限公司